Writing
THE ROUTES

Writing
THE ROUTES

Bus poems and stories
from Albuquerque

Dante M. Berry

Writing the Routes: Bus poems and stories from Albuquerque
Copyright ©2015 Dante M. Berry

ISBN: 978-1-940769-40-0
Publisher: Mercury HeartLink
Printed in the United States of America

Book design by Mercury HeartLink
www.heartlink.com, editor@heartlink.com

Mercury HeartLink
www.heartlink.com

Contents

MORNING LIGHT

FIRST LADY AND HAIKUS

MID-DAY JAUNTS

COMANCHE PONY

GOING HOME

MID-SEPTEMBER MOURNING

ACKNOWLEDGMENTS

The first poetic voice I heard was my mother's. She is the story teller in me.

I recognize my Belen high school English teachers, Muriel Smith, Adrian Brody, Edwina Chavez-Gardner, and Connie Decker. These women cultivated and brought out in me the desire to write years ago. The seeds they planted are growing.

I thank the Fixed and Free poetry community and the Rio Grande Valencia Poets group for their support and encouragement.

Special thanks to Richard Berry, Billy Brown, Mark Fleisher, Damien Flores, Jules Nyquist, Andrea Penner, Joe Sandoval, Donna J. Snyder, Marion Subjenski, John Taylor, Kuan Tikun, and Stewart Warren.

Cover photography and photographs of the author by Andrew Kozeliski: combining the beauty of nature with the structure of the manmade world. *kozphotos.com*

Illustrations by John Barney; John is an artist and poet living in Albuquerque, NM. His latest work deals with the Rio Grande Silvery Minnow. John Baaney: *humusmirabilis@live.com*.

Margaret, my beloved wife, beautiful woman, devoted to family and a lover of life, you have been my faithful companion since our journey began as teen-agers.

Ramon, I think of you every day.

Delilah, you inspired me to write when I was mourning.

This book is dedicated to the drivers of ABQ RIDE, City of Albuquerque Transit Department. They are dedicated public servants who get people safely to their destinations and many are grateful for their service.

INTRODUCTION

Metaphorically we all travel through life. In my case it's been on a series of buses, contemplating the scenery, and as I matured, the changing seasons of life and death. I've been a bus rider for almost 50 years. School buses, charter, city and double decker buses too. I've ridden them all. As an introvert, my journey has been primarily in silence, sitting in middle-row window seats, but that changed for me the summer of 2013.

I experienced a series of profound personal losses between 1995 and 1997. It began with the suicide of my teen-aged nephew. This shocked the entire family. His mother, my sister-in-law, spiraled into a deep depression. A few months later on Mother's Day she took her life. To this day, late night or early morning phone calls trigger a reaction in me. Tragedy struck again in June of that same year, this time closer to my heart. While on vacation in San Diego my youngest brother, age 25, drowned saving my 10 year old daughter from a rip-tide current. The incredible blow of it all sent me into depression. I wanted to go away, take a long retreat, but life would not allow it. I was the head of the family, provider for eight children and a wife and we were remodeling a home. There was no time to grieve. My poor mother was an emotional wreck and my father, at age 78, was heartbroken. As the eldest son it fell on me to make the funeral arrangements. I hated that duty! My father was part of the Great Generation, a World War II veteran. It's ironic that on Veterans Day 1996 he suffered a massive stroke that left him speechless and paralyzed on his right side. I often think, in some way, the death of his youngest son brought about the stroke. Each of these heartbreaks took a toll on me and my family, but the biggest blow was yet to come.

A beautiful October day in 1997. Over the valley Sandhill cranes sang their songs of return as hot air balloons blossomed in the sky. On this day my oldest son drove away and never came back. Ramon was killed in a horrific head-on collision. The tremendous impact killed him instantly. I recall searching the crash site days later and finding part of his wrist watch some 60 feet from the point of impact. This was the gift I'd given him for his 15th birthday, only eight months prior.

The image of his broken necrosed body on the mortuary table is forever burned into my memory. Wanting to spare my wife such an unpleasant sight, I arranged for her to say goodbye to her baby after his body had been placed in a black vinyl burial bag, only his right hand visible from the black cocoon of death. She held and kissed that hand again and again. It was surreal. We cried like a hard New Mexico rain. The torrent of emotional pain and its effects on me and the whole family still unfold.

I first became aware of my seasonal anxiety during the fall of 2003. It seemed every September and October I'd engage in self-destructive behavior. A counselor helped me make this connection in 2010. So, in subsequent years I began "healthy" projects that carried me through October. One year I build a tree house for the grandchildren. In 2013 my wife and I began preparing for a backpacking trip to Spain. We'd planned to walk the Camino de Santiago during September and October. During the summer months, as part of my preparation, I carried a pack. Inside were my son's scrap book and photo albums. The memories weighed almost 20 pounds, a load I carried slung over my shoulder, and in my mind, as I walked to and from bus stops and on the trek home from the train station.

On my commute to work, I'd go through the memory books and allow myself to grieve. Finally, after years of keeping it all within, I allowed myself to mourn, not afraid to let others see my pain. When people saw me emotional I would explain why and show them photographs. To my surprise, everyone was supportive and this gave me strength. This also happened with one of the bus drivers, in August of 2013. I shared with her the story of my son's death. She listened and offered her sympathy and healing smile. I started talking to the driver and we became acquainted. Occasionally I stayed on to the end of the route. Then I'd walk to work carrying my memories, but my load seemed lighter. Discovering this opening to people and sharing my feelings was new and pleasant for me. When the time came for her to bid on a new route, I said I'd write a poem for her as a parting gift. This became the first of my bus poems. Inspired by this driver I have found a creative outlet and I am grateful to her. Since then I have made it a point to talk to people and get to know the drivers. I have written poems for several of them. There are some 40 bus routes in the transit system. I've ridden them and composed poems for all, plus a few more. Riding the routes is enjoyable and the experiences provide lots to write about.

In November of 2014 the idea gelled to complete a book about people and events on city buses. I decided I'd write a poem for each route in the ABQ Ride system. Many of the poems are based on actual events and people. Poems are dedicated to drivers, bus passengers or people special in my life. A tragic thread runs through the collection, yet there is also humor and light hearted verse. The short stories are also inspired from my bus riding experiences and personal life.

Albuquerque is a wonderful city, and I have gotten to know it better by riding the routes. This collection of prose and poetry is dedicated to the public servants of the transit department, some of whom have become friends. Writing, I have found, is a powerful outlet for my emotions, helping me to heal. My autumn project for 2015 is this book.

೫ ೫ ೫ ೫ ೫

ONE

Morning Light

Rail Runner, Gasping Pale

The pen I was given at the summer writers workshop, is running out of ink. I think that's good. It means I've been writing on my daily commute. Interestingly, the pen has become an old friend to me - A friend I keep close to my heart.

Alas, only partial words appear now. They start black then grow faint in mid-phrase. Out of respect for my old friend I let the pen write to its end. Though these final words make little sense. Now the ballpoint only presses into paper. Ghost writing. It's gasping. I panic, scribble in the margin trying to revive it. No use. My friend is gone.

Pausing, I look at my workmate in my hand - the work we've done. I sigh, and think about this pen gone dry, a poet who has no more to say. Who, out of words, gasps the last phrase. No more breath. The ink of life expelled. Ashen eyelids closed, the poet's face pallid, his body in a casket. In his breast pocket his favorite pen. Both are laid to rest.

ROUTE #222-2, GOLDEN LIGHT

For Delilah

Looking east, Sandias silhouette
against pale skies.
Laced in golden glimmer
by the sunrise they hide,
cloudy monsoon remnants
cling to rocky peaks.

Black, high-backed
air adjusted chair
set perfectly to balance
thinking waiting there.
She checks mirrors,
each face in place
train pulls away our ride begins.

Short sleeved uniform
maroon with golden lettering.
Black shorts, shoes with low cut socks reveal,
skin tones – Mediterranean.
Perhaps a great granddaughter
of Sephardic origin.

Bicyclist legs, toned and strong
flex to work the pedals.
Tanned hands command
a rolling cage of twenty tons.

Rumbling steadily up Gibson,
early golden light
beaming through the window
illuminates her face
like an icon Madonna
wearing Ray-Ban shades.

Café con leche colored,
adorned with silver ring
wide lips glisten.
Hair pulled up and fun
brown and auburn fountain
golden high lights catch the sun.

Consistent, carful, courteous
avoiding dips and bumps
thinking and adjusting,
timing every light
the route she runs.

Pull the cord, go our way,
thanks, most riders say.
Poised, acknowledging each person.
Reserved not often smiling,
but when she does,
a perfect strand of pearls revealed
beautiful and bright, a joy to see.
My prayer for her to always be
safe and well in golden light.
                   Amen.

Route #31, Turnstiles

For those who work at Sandia Laboratories

Faces clipped to clothes
approach in rows and pause
before the spindled gate.

Black oxide strip a key
swipe reveals identity.
Four-note micro-symphony.

The turnstile clicks
one is scooped in.
Before the gate all are equal.

ROUTE #96, MORNING MARIA

For working immigrants

One September morning she got on.
He watched her from his seat, attracted
by her colors. Her hair, eyes and skin
all natural and brown. Shades of gentle
brown. Soft like her demeanor
meant to blend in.

She was in the middle of her summer,
he beginning autumn.
They shared a space each morning
along with others. He admired
her dedication. Her job was here,
her heart apart from Mexico.

Their morning rendezvous became
a motivator for him to be on time.
He helped her with English,
loved to hear her speak.
Her accent was intriguing,
her answers intelligent.

Morning friendship grew, exchanging
gifts at Christmas. Exchanging pieces
of their lives. Hopes and fears intersected
on a bus to unknown destination.

One Tuesday morning she was gone.
He never saw her again. He learned
she'd been deported.

His autumn heart broke open.
Months past, he still checks the corner
where she once got on. He thinks,
How many Marias are in Mexico?
Just one.

ROUTE #155, NORTHWEST TRANSIT CENTER, ICE CAPADES

For Ralph

It arrived at night, slippery semi-clear, air entombed
in little spheres.
Deceptive layers coat roads and bridges. A bitter appetite
Winter's saliva does consume cars and trucks; slide sideways
into fences down ravines there abandoned till day light.

Flyover freeways in suspended animation wrapped in cold blue sky.
Traffic cops block off and on ramps, shut down river bridges.
Tepid drivers fidget ending up marooned against concrete blocks.
People walk faster than the 155 stuck in line, tail pipe breathing.

Detours restrict the traffic flow, backed up a mile
at Coors and I-40.
Rapid Rides in line three deep creep from
the Northwest Transit Center.
Two-hour delay a gaffe. Winter guffaws again, licks its lips
settles in and watches the show on a February Friday morning.

ROUTE #34, GUARDIAN ANGEL

For Michael and all the protectors, the extra board drivers

Native
of the clouds,
great defender,
protector of the board.
Oh, Michael, Archangel
Long black hair, thick strong bones.
We are not alone for you are present.
If fatigue or illness come
you from clouds descend
and drive our route.
Give us rest,
Amen.

ROUTE #50, GREY SKY RHYTHM

For Ray

Languid April rain
tapping on a panoramic windshield.
A jet accelerates into grey mist.

Thirty inch long wiper blades
glide across a view of the West Side.
Engine rumble, gargles fuel.

West on Martin Luther King,
the rain sings gently of his courage.
Pass the old Saint Joe's, now loves you less.

It's a shame, the city needs more rain,
the driver speaks over his shoulder.
Adjusts a knob and hissss.

Vacuum changes the rhythm
of the blades. Rhythmic work
remains the same. People, bus go on.

ROUTE #94, UNSER BOULEVARD

For the drivers out of Daytona

Dad was furious when he found out.

What the hell were you thinking?
They clocked you doing 120 miles an hour.
At that speed you'll cause an accident.
Do you want to be responsible for that?

All I could do was shrug.
Dad shook his head and said,
If you can't average at least 160
you ain't got what it takes!

These are Indy cars junior, understand?

Old Bus 302

For the Drivers out of Yale

Charles, Steve and Mr. Brown
were warming up at five a.m.
in the Yale garage,
burning fuel out their rear ends.

He's an old timer, his odometer
reads over six hundred thousand miles,
Steve explains in admiration.

I heard they're going to get old timers
and sell their body parts.
Then what's left they'll melt down.

Ah, hell no, Charles, who told you that?
He's not getting cremated,
he's going south to Mexico.
You know, escort señritas, carry folks with chickens,
and transport kids to their escuelas.

Mr. Brown goes on, the others listen.
He may be worn, but he's still rolling.
He's gonna get a whole new suit,
green and red spray-painted stripes,
maybe a Lady of Guadalupe tattoo.
Heck, down there mechanics fix you up
and it don't cost an arm and a tire either.
Yes sir, in Mexico a dollar goes a long way.

Skeptical, Charles's brake line hisses.

I've got to go, if I'm late they'll fire me.
I doubt they will, don't worry,
says Steve, his eyes focused.
The buses honk, pulling out into the street
to start their morning routes.

Mr. Brown, he stuck around
to get it straight from 302
and maybe start to plan
his own southbound retreat.

ROUTE# 141, A MOTHER'S LOVE

A mother travels to District Court to sort out legal matters
involving her two boys.

Woman, with two sons,
casualties to drugs,
stands before the judge
seated
on a wooden throne
sworn
to justice.

On either side a son is crucified
by needles of addiction.
She pleads on their behalf.

> *A los pies de Jesus*
> *las tres Marias lloran*
> *muy amargamente*
> *mientre*
> *la madre*
> *de los ladrones*
> *pide perdon al juez*

A mother suffers seeing
sons decay into street,
I beg you, keep my son in prison
at least it may save one.

The son on the left turned away.
The one on the right faced the judge
and said, *Remember me.*

Route #251, Snow Queen

For Lionides

The snow queen rides the train
    early in the morning.
        puts on makeup without a mirror.

Snow has fallen on the valley.
    Albuquerque glistens
        before daybreak.

The covering of snow, makeup
    makes all beautiful,
        at least for a while
            all is new.

Old rusted cars just disappear
    crippled fatigued frame
        tattered trampoline
            looks OK in white.

A person's ugly past like
    bottles, bags, and cans
        a trash strewn yard,
            of abuse.

She rides the train then bus to work,
    beauty secrets kept
        in a leopard skin handbag
            and silver case.

Snow queen, cosmetologist.
    Applies facial beauty
        helps other heal inside.

Her hands trained
        to put on her face
            without a mirror.

Survival skill she learned.
        Shield from verbal abuse
            developed long ago.

Now she helps others
    feel good
        about themselves
            like snow can do
                for a while.

Route #790, College Conversations

For all students

From west side to UNM
the blue line runs true.
At Cottonwood Mall
young riders dash.

Back packs and sacks bounce
to make a connection.
The accordion bus waits, it happens
every day this way.

Bus conversations,
about social experiments.

Toys distributed to girls,
trucks of every color.
Barbie Dolls given
to boys to play.
By the second day
boys made armies with Barbies
          while girls
arranged trucks into families,
 mama, dad and kids.

Political correctness is washed up.

Young minds postulate,
free speech debates.

Siamese twin buses
joined at the middle
pivots off Lomas onto
                    Girard.
Students off,
to the classroom world.
Backpacks and sacks bounce
            to get there on time.

Route #53, Mother Groomed

South on Isleta past Gun Club Road
dew on fields catch morning glow.

Spring comes with promises of green.
In response, the ground is groomed.

Spades turn, hoes form rows, like braids
in mother's loam brown hair.

On hands and knees, beads woven in,
treasured beans, chile, corn, and melons.

Ever watchful father sun smiles bright
his laughter growing with the days.

Water from *acequias* anoints her braids.
Liquid shimmer soaks into soil and seed.

Twin offspring born, root and shoot set free.
One pale clings to mother, the other jade reaches for light.

Earth and sun, work and dreams all green
traveling down Isleta in the spring.

Route #3 Replaced by Harmony

For Stewart

Who are we
if not a trinity.
Self-perception, what others see and actuality.
Harmony is,
the trinity in one.

Route #98, Cathartic Lenses

For Ginny

Reading through weeping,
eyes blink forming
tiny splashes of tears
that dry on the back side of glasses.
Specs, smears, translucent spots,
the residue of a good poem
wiped clean by an untucked shirt.

TWO

First Lady and Haikus

THE FIRST LADY OF TRANSIT

A nickname, but also a title of honor belonging to Patty Sandoval, bus driver for the City of Albuquerque. Patty is the first woman in Transit Department history to earn the top spot on the bus driver seniority list. There are more than 220 Motor-coach Operators in the Transit Department. Today, about 20 percent are women, not the case in 1990 when Patty joined the ranks. It's taken hard work, dedication and good health to reach the top. Patty retired December 2014 with 25 years of public service.

On a Wednesday morning run, I watch as she shuttles citizens of the Duke City from the foothills of the Sandia Mountains to the northwest transit center near Cibola High School. Puddles from the night's monsoon rain appear as odd shaped mirrors on black asphalt. Cars occasionally shatter them into droplets. Waiting passengers step back from the spray.

Patty's professionalism is easy to see. She greets passengers, answers questions, checks mirrors for traffic and stays on time. During the commute a senior citizen wearing a Vietnam service cap is concerned he will miss his connection with the eastbound Montgomery bus. Patty radios dispatch and assures her rider he will make the connection. With a slight limp, he walks back to his seat, thankful.

At the end of the line there is a 10- minute break. Patty enjoys a cigarette while telling me a little about herself. She was born in Des Moines, New Mexico, the third of four daughters. Growing up on a ranch she learned the value of hard work, often helping her father doing boys' chores.

Patty is tall and slender, her skin light brown with golden undertones, like the caramel on flan. A thin gold chain with a cross hangs from her neck, a testament to her faith. She is a bundle of energy, walking around inspecting her bus, chewing gum all the time talking to me while checking her watch. I ask if she lives by the clock. She scowls then smiles and says, "It's a chinga!"

Patty drove school and charter buses for 16 years before joining the City. "When I started in 1990 there were only six or seven lady drivers," she explains. Any harassment? She pauses, draws on her cigarette, "For the most part all the male drivers have been very nice." I probe, but she affirms no negative attitudes or comments directed at her through the years. If there were, she's not telling.

What about work hours? She's worked every shift possible, splits, late nights, but prefers morning straights. On a typical work day she is up before 4 a.m. and operating a bus by 5:40 a.m.

Back behind the wheel, Patty lays a towel across her lap. She explains it serves as an apron protecting her uniform from dirty seatbelts. Patty takes pride in her appearance and dress. Her shirt and short pants are clean and ironed. She wears ankle socks trimmed in white lace and her black shoes are polished. "We get a monthly uniform allowance, but it's barely enough by the time you pay for your patches," she tells me. "We haven't had a pay raise in five years. Really it's up to us to make our uniforms last."

As we head east across Montaño Bridge she tells me she enjoys the outdoors, camping and fishing. She plans to do both once she retires. The following day, I ask other drivers about Patty. She is well known even among the rookies. She works hard and always says hello to everyone, one driver tells me. "She's a sweetheart," said one of the lady drivers. Her peers admire her positive attitude and outgoing character. Her dedication and work ethic earn her the respect of other drivers.

She truly is the First Lady of Transit.

The Fleet Haikus

For the mechanics

300 series

worn gray charcoal seats
the old fleet sits more people
together, we age

700 and 900 series

garnet saddle seats
outside skin is bay, black, white
city work horses

600 series

green inside and out
seats on two levels, fine views
see past and future

THREE
Mid-day Jaunts

ROUTE #1, RAB - DAYS LIKE THESE

For Ramon

On days like today
I marvel at creation
I feel the warm low-angled sun
Inhale an azure sky
Cranes sing songs again
Gentle breeze kiss
Hot air balloons float by
Like memories of love

On days like today
When New Mexico is
The land of enchantment
Gardens still producing
The smell of chile roasting
Soccer fields still green
Echoing with children

On days like today
The most beautiful of all
I am often sad, sober, somber
And the beauty of it all
Is subdued pain inside
For on a day just like today
You drove away and died.

ROUTE #8, WAITING

For bus people who patiently wait

Caution yellow markings on top.
Black, bulbous, fig-shaped abdomen
fades to grim velvet underside.
Her one-inch long appendages bent.
Still, perfect symmetry on silk.
Mesmerizing, bobs in the breeze
on invisible quilt she weaves.
In time, wind will stir up a meal.

ROUTE #11, FAT CARS

For Manny

European cars
Come to America
Get bigger, grow fat
Hey, what's up with that?
Just take a look at
The Mini Cooper
Now a super Cooper
Fiat 500
Now 500L – Large
What's going on?
It must be the gas
Abundant fast-food stations
Enticing corner stores
Compete to offer more
Junk-food fuel galore
Corn ethanol blends
High fructose gasoline
Little cars start lean
But then lose will power
Consume too much benzene
Similar to these
Japanese cars grew
In the 80's and 90's too
It's a disturbing trend
Soon, Smart Cars will be
Fat dumb and happy.

Route #140, Tax Collector

For the poor and homeless of the city

Mathew, was a tax collector.
Standing at his post
                    he was despised,
like some who ride the Little Central.

Onboard every bus, a tax collector stands
at the entrance,
                    stainless steel tower
silent, stoic it demands.

Gray plastic mouth on a flat head,
the fare box digests
                    coins and paper.
If you want to ride pay, or walk.

Bundled in old clothes a woman pays
using thirty-five
                    small copper coins.
She shuffles back to the nearest seat.

I tell you she has put in more
than all the rest
                    who gave from their surplus.
San Mateo, bless the poor who ride today.

ROUTE #10, FOURTH STREET SEASONS

For Margaret

If the year were but a day

Spring begins each morning
Growing light, unfolding buds
A baby's coo like doves
Awaiting dawn in branches

Mid-day an endless summer
Young lovers in their prime
Ample time to strive and thrive
Canopies thick dark green
Teeming with life and laughter

Deep green yields to orange brown
Evening shadows stain the ground
Autumn's breath is misty gold
Foils fall in colors bold
All creation growing old

Skeleton trees stand alone
Winter's night begets bone
Waning moon casts mournful glow
Casket's pall made of snow

Underneath, the hope of spring.

Route #16-18, Last Ride

The 16-18 bus, what a relaxing trip.
It cuts through the city, from heights, down into valley,
hoods with no money to places with plenty.
What else cuts through you, eclectic Duke City,
never discriminating: age, race, rich or poor.
Starts with a taste of hard candy, smack, *chiva*, shit.

On a balmy August day, young *Nuevomexicano*
boards the bus, floating, sits in back, cool air soothing.
The family avoids him, locking doors behind him.
Hearts hard, broken open from lies, deceptions, stealing.
He hates what he's doing, but hates more the craving.
Pin prick, push, tingling rush of ecstasy, it's done.

The 16-18, so relaxing, city scenes
roll past like scrolling color iPhone memories.
Eyes closing, letting go, breaths weaken like a match
goes from flame to plume under a spoon, used up.
Somewhere along the way, between getting off and
getting on, a soul pulls *Stop Requested*.

Alvarado Transfer Station, people walk off.
He's still sleeping there in back, says a passenger.
Slumped face in sun, driver feels for breath, there is none.
Young Chicano took a trip, a dimes's worth was his fare
Was it redrum or just a plain OD, who cares.
Someone always does, cries, prays, tries to understand.

A young man overdosed on an ABQ bus on a Wednesday afternoon, A tragic death, victim to heroin addiction; a modern plague that does not discriminate. This poem is dedicated to the memory of so many who were loved and prayed for and could not overcome.

Route #36, Armored Transport

For Gloria

People; people of every kind,
the city's greatest asset
transported in a twenty-two ton
virtual steel vault.

Coin and currency in their pockets,
jewelry, every type
adorn their body,
turquoise, silver, pearls and gold.

Bilingual former armored guard
licensed to carry a .38 and .45,
but her favorite is a shotgun
just because it's fun.

Safe point end-to-end solution.
Buses carry people
Burque's prized possession
driven by a former
pistol-packing woman
with a smile.

Route #40, D-Bus Goes Round

For John

> **Summer** monsoon rains, **Fall**
> on white cotton like **Winter**
> snow melts into **Spring**
> runoff and ...

Route #53 – 5, Deep Summer South

For José

At Bridge, turn and venture into deep south.
The city sheds its skin, and strip malls stop.
Fluid brown, *acequias* flow east and south.
Llanterias, produce stands, alfalfa crops.

The city sheds its grip, and strip malls stop.
Bronze, Sargent Julian Narvaez stands watch.
Carnecerias, produce stands, and garden crops.
An original stretch of Route 66.

Bronze, Sargent Julian Narvaez stands strong.
Italian nuns care for *inocentes.*
Drive along a stretch of original Route 66.
Trailer drives by, alfalfa stacked six high.

Los inocentes and Canossian Nuns.
Isleta, as far south as transit goes.
Verdant pastures, gorgeous horses run.
Pajarito, Los Padillas, Malpais Road, stop.

Route #66, Unbridled Spirits

For Copper

These cheeses complement the wine Jesus
made from well water, but that's a hard sell.

Poor chosen people, share this bottle of ripple
drink the pain away again my brown brethren.

Unbridled breasts, brunette and blondes market spirits
because all sorts of spectator sports go better with booze.

It's sad when beer ads preach responsible drinking
while CEOs make millions and millions irresponsibly.

Some spend for a fine Bordeaux blend $500 per bottle.
Napa valley cult wineries like Jesus healing the planet
                              through miraculous wine.

Route #66-4, Captain Jack Sparrow

For Nick

Captain Jack Sparrow
got kicked off the bus
twin braided chin and all.

The pirate got on
wild-eyed, his mind a little off.
His compass does not point north
                              of course.

Jack swaggered back,
sprawled out on the seats.
Turned out his compass was a lighter.
T'was cigarette smoke he breathed.

You can't smoke in here, declared the driver.
Hey, it's OK, I'll put it out.
The driver put HIM out, and Jack Sparrow
                              blew away.

ROUTE #66-5, TRANSIT MEDITATION

For Armando

The guru on the mountain city hall
approved of kneeling buses.
In the temples of Yale and Daytona
buses knelt and prayed
for a sixty-five cent raise.

Meanwhile, city budgeteers
deep in meditation
received a revelation.
Ahmm, more modern machines
let us approve machines
for them instead.

And so a new green fleet
of yoga buses was commissioned.
These yoga buses will increase stretch and relaxation while reducing stress
and work induced frustration.

On Central, buses have been seen
laying on their backs, releasing natural gas.
Concerned citizens dial 311 and ask,
are they drunk or is it shavasana*?

Shavasana, a yoga position.

Route #66-6, Anima Mia

For those battling addictions of every kind

It seems my being
is hostage on a bus
driven by a demon
with blood shot eyes.

My soul trapped sits in back.
The chime cord is broken hope.
Occasionally I glance up
at the red LED board.
The date reads eternity.

I stare outside, forehead
imprisoned by glass.
Where are we, I ask.
No reply, bizarre scenery blurs by.
Was that my stop? I shout.
Ignored, I sit, hands clasped.

At last the motor coach operator's
sulfur voice booms back,
Shut up, don't pray.
I'm the driver now,
this route never ends.

Route #97, Zuni Rd. Physics Lesson

Front page caption reads,
"*City Bus Slams Into House*"

Red means stop, on green you go,
basic law of traffic flow.
What goes up, must come down.
Coal goes up, Lead comes down.
Zuni forms where they meet up.

A white van heading south,
weighs about five thousand pounds.
City bus commuting east
green machine weighs twenty tons.
Fixed on a foundation, a corner home sits
pine wood frame, brown stucco skin.
Wham!
Under the load of impact pressure
solid glass behaves as liquid
shattered droplets spray in air.
Metal yields, deforms plastic.
Drastic crash, a little earthquake.

Eight people, too, part of the equation.
Like sub-atomic particles
released in the collision.
Kinetic energy transfer, billiard balls collide.
White van, green bus, brown home,
women rolls
into kitchen corner pocket,
screaming.

Time, a second sure does matter
difference between nothing or disaster.
After the dust all settles,
insurance rubrics and lawyers.
Hey, now that's some funky physics.

Route #198, Hear This Prayer

For the Gathering of Nations

It all matters when it's a prayer.
Everything, each color, every bead
and pattern, each step and drumbeat
has a meaning, every bird song praise.

Porcupine quills woven
into ear hoops and painted
adorn, caress the brown skin
of a native princess.

Hoops hang,
blue mountain bands, white cloud,
red berries, orange sun.
All these, you see, are litanies.

Route #36-2, Canoeing Down Rio

For Leroy

Hermanita (little sister)
begins at Alameda
then gently heads south.

Starts narrow,
just two lanes,
growing wider
as she meanders
passed remnant farms
towards old town.

The road mimics sister's path,
just a little to the west,
as best she can
with gentle turns and curves
trees kiss homes to families.

Past Griegos she widens into boulevard,
now Rio Grande.
Both Lady of Guadalupe
and Nahalat Shalom
grow just off her waterside.

Casitas are willows along the bank.
Las casas mas grande
are stately cottonwoods or
tall prolific elms,
legacy of Clyde Tingly.

Between Candelaria and Campbell
fire station number 10 can pass
for a pueblo style home,
with bright red chile paint
around a large garage door.

Roads branch west to the *bosque* trails.
Roads grow like Floral, Lilac and Rose.
Now pass under I-40,
modern day Camino Real.
Little sister arrives at old town,
but ends up
at the country club.

ROUTE #2-3, WATCH THE VIDEO

Reality T.V. –
drivers watch it every day
through the big screen window of a bus.
When the drama gets out of hand
we can watch the bus-cam
           on a smart phone.

On Friday June the fifth,
a man claims to be a cop
at a stop on Eubank.
Expired bus pass
comments get crass on camera.
His anger a sharpened dagger
in his hand.
Throws a blow, assaults the driver.

Minutes later, on foot
suitcase in tow
police apprehend
the angry man
and give him a free ride.

That face behind the wheel
is a servant not a target
for entitled anger.
Mace, stones thrown at close range,
punches, spit, insults of all kinds.

Public servants deserve gratitude
not the violent attitude
                    of a few
who's antics we can view
on a cell phone video.

Route #766, Working Others

For health care workers

The mechanic at the shop
Fixes cars and reassembles autos
In his back yard cars are parked three deep
A muscle car will atrophy sitting up on blocks

And what about the plumber?
He fixes leaks and unclogs pipes for others
When resting in his den, he will not budge
To stop the drip that's driving his spouse nuts

The physical therapist
She releases muscles, eases pains for others
Coaches people to regain lost motion
Who takes care of her when she needs a back rub?

.

FOUR
Comanche Pony

Route #13, Comanche Pony

Introduction

On Comanche heading east at sunset
the appearance of the mountain changes,
a transition from blue to pale red glow.
Female driver's long dark hair, catches light.
I delight in the display before me.
A yellow moon over the Sandias.
The 700 - series bus colors
bay, tan, black, white, like a painted pony.
On Comanche at the end of the day,
the colors and sights combine in my mind.
I drift and leave reality behind.

Prologue

Father named me Yellow Moon.
I tell this sacred story to honor him
and my brave mothers. Their actions
saved my son and freed me to a new life.

The year was nineteen hundred and three
when I rode away on the Comanche pony,
saving my son from the mouth of the snake.
Ancient serpent our people kept secret.
Snake deity inscribed on black boulders,
sacrifice and punishment worshiped still.
We the Sky People, proud, independent,
warriors who held fast to traditions,
our ceremonies in phase with seasons.
New ideas brought both hope and fear.
Primal rites fought back against changing times.

But love, courage, faith and foresight overcame.

Hunting

Father began to prepare me
when I at twelve began changing into a woman.
"My husband, why must you take her hunting?
She should be obedient, helping me,
learning traditions from her grandmother.
She is our only daughter and changing,
and elders question what you are doing."
"Yes woman, she is our only daughter,
but she is strong and our world is changing.
Old ways are passing. "

Father was wise and knew that he was right.
Mother was strong and not afraid to fight.
Grandmother's actions defused the tension
as she gently stroked mother's long black hair.
The bond of beauty we shared, our long hair.
Our mantle of strength.

It was a large hunting party,
many uncles, cousins and sons,
some with old bows and arrows.
Together with loyal dogs and horses
all journeyed eastward for the hunt.
Father, proud, confidant walked by my side.
Resilient, deflecting piercing stares.

I ate less than boys and was just as fast.
Each day I faced challenges and testing.
Unaware, scrutiny surrounded me.

It was my great adventure
lasting a month and a lifetime.
Father instructed me in many things:
how to find water, reading signs on the ground,
which plants could be eaten,
and how to chip a point from stone.

From a high ridge he showed me old and new.
Volcano hills where our people inscribed
stories, signs and symbols from long ago.
In the distance smoke-breath of an iron horse
traveling with speed to future places.
Beyond the great river he pointed out
blue mountains, and at their base people lived.
People as countless as the leaves
of an old cotton wood tree.
On Christianity and old rites, he shed light,
pointing out old and new he explained change.
I cherished the wisdom he gave.

Evenings at the fire were for storytelling,
knowledge sharing and planning.
Scouts spotted herds of many antelope,
several on the plains near the canyon's edge.
Some spoke in favor of hunting them one by one.
Among our group we had three iron guns.
Discussions brewed between old and new ways.
Father spoke, "It's not old or new.
We must decide what works best.
We could harvest many using old techniques,
our precious bullets saved for other hunts."

Elder hunters eagerly explained the plan;
stone wall funnel used by our ancestors.
Running is useful also for hunting.
All Sky People run. We were instructed
and shown what to do.

The following day, hunters on horseback
began the stampede. Runners positioned
along the way channeled the antelope
into the funnel. From behind rocks
I watched the dust cloud approach.
We were to jump out running and shouting
from the sides, a final scare over the edge.
Hunger the consequence of failure.

The shouts of men and barking of dogs
mixed with rumble of hooves, all charging ahead.
Pronghorn rushing, nostrils flaring, wide eyes,
my heart pounding energy through my veins.
I jumped out at full speed, yelling, angling
into the frantic herd from the left side.
One followed by others tried to cut back.
Determined I flashed my teeth and charged them.
They leapt into air as though they might fly.
Graceful they fell, swallowed by the canyon.

We all yelped shouts of triumph and great joy.
It was a bountiful harvest of meat and skins.
Some hunters on horseback smiled at me.
"This one is yours," father said, then with two
poles tied to my waist, because I was strong,
I pulled to the top my antelope prize

alongside the boys.

That night around the fire was ancient.
The burning cedar cracking in delight
cast an ancient glow. Our teeth gleamed orange
as we spoke stories of the fruitful hunt.
Some spoke of carving images on the
black volcano stones.

The success and excitement of that first hunt
for me were not repeated again.
In the following years the boys became
stronger and faster. They no longer looked
at me as equal, but as a woman.

Shepherd Boy

Almost sixteen, I was quite capable.
I could hunt and track! I felt left behind,
relegated to cook and fetch water.
I had a helper, Little Song her name.
Together with old uncle and his dog,
we maintained camp for the hunting party.
Our hunting group this time was smaller,
three men with sons all with hunting rifles.
Caused by changing times, factions formed
along lines of tradition. Some placed blame
for hardships on others because they allowed
Spanish and Anglo ways.
Divisions among the clans grew wider.

Nestled behind junipers, our camp
just two hills away from flowing water.

It was early morning, birds still stirring
when I knelt to wash my face, and saw him.
He was young and sinewy, his color
reddish brown like core wood of a cedar.
He greeted me in Tiwa, I frowned.
Raising his hand he tried a strange tongue.
I only stared back.
Coming forward he smiled at me and now,
in Spanish said, "Your hair is beautiful."
I felt my face flush.

In two deft hops he crossed the stream to me.
His eyes were spectacular, golden brown,
a trace of green, the like I'd never seen.

"Your long dark hair reminds me of my horse."
I felt made fun of and I knew he could tell.
"I mean to say, my horse is beautiful.
I mean...," his words were stones to stumble on.
He paused, regained his composure, then spoke,
"I'm sure you'd like to see my loyal horse."
I only nodded.
Happy, he said, "Come back at midday,
I'll have the pony here."
He hopped to the other side and was gone.

We gathered wood and cooked, the morning passed.
At noon I took the pails to fetch water.
"Can I come with you?" Little Song called out.
"No! You must keep old uncle company,
when I get back I'll take you to find nuts."

He was sitting in the shade of willows.
Spotting me he shouted, "Come and see her."
She was a beautiful painted horse,
strong and sleek, her colors bay, black and white.
My hands stroked her face and she nuzzled back.
"She is wonderful."
"You see, it was a compliment I gave."
"Yes, it was, thank you."
"Her name is Estrella, for the star mark
on her head, and her loyalty to me
is like a friendly star shining at night."

"Is she a fast runner?"
"She's fast enough, her real strength
is her endurance.
If I ask her she'll go fifty miles."
I only smiled, then asked, "Can I ride her?"
"Yes, she likes you."
He put me on her back,
my first ride, the feeling stimulating.
He walked alongside us and asked my name.
"I say my name Kochini Tawadza,
it means Yellow Moon.
When I was born, my father saw it rising.
I was given a Christian name as well,
Clare, like the loyal friend of St. Francis."

"What is your name?"
He answered, "Ezekiel"
"Does it have meaning?"
"It means God's strength."
"That is a good name." I smiled at him.

"Is your village nearby?"
He shook his head.
"What are you doing here Ezekiel?"
"I tend sheep for my father, our camp is
on the other side of that rocky ridge.
Our home, a town called Tome, is miles away.
And why are you here?"
"My family is hunting in these hills."
There was a long pause.

We gathered our thoughts.
"I must be going back now, old uncle
will be wondering where I am."
His strong hands on my hips lifted me off.
Faces close, we blushed.
"Will you return tomorrow morning?"

I smiled at him.
Little Song talked, asking many questions.
Half listening, I helped her gather piñon,
my mind and heart on the shepherd boy.
Little Song asked, "Are you not feeling well?"
I looked at her and said, "Why do you ask?
"You've been collecting deer droppings not nuts."
I looked into my basket, she was right.
We began to laugh so hard we cried.

Sleep a thin veil only, my mind active,
with thoughts of him, mixed with swirling visions
of the painted pony.
At last, rescued by the pale morning.

Birds sang sweet love songs with the coming day,
sitting in the cool we listened to them.
Holding my hand he said, "I have to leave,
I must move the flocks, but promise to return."
We agreed to meet in late afternoon.

The hunting group had come and gone again.
The arching sun seemed slow, the work was long.
At last with all meat cut the time arrived
and I set off jogging to go see him.
"Sister, where do you go?"
"To get water." I shouted back.
"But you have no pail."
I turned and ran back. There she stood
smiling at me puzzled, head tilted like a puppy.
Excited, my heart pumping energy,
as in pursuit of prey, I ran to him.

Giddy, we began to play, chasing like children,
then ending like woman and man,
falling in love on the stream bank,
sand was our marriage bed, shade our thin sheet.
Our bodies embraced, sleep overcame us.
The sun had set, only an orange glow
my light as I ran back, dizzy in love.

Secret Harvest
Once it was home for two growing families,
father's relatives.
Influenza came claiming the lives
of all four children.
The brokenhearted parents moved away.
Now a spacious place occupied by four.
Father was a council member
so our place accepted, though there were some
among the village who were envious.

Our home had two levels and three large rooms,
the largest for cooking and gathering.
The back third of the ground floor, living space
where I slept and grandmother lived as well.
Above us, mother and father's chamber
accessed using an old white pine ladder.
The roof top outside my parent's chamber
used for drying our food and a lookout.
Designed for defense, our windows narrow,
large enough for ample light, yet
wide enough for a child to escape.

It was harvest time.
Late summer green gave way to yellow brown.
Corn and squash drying alongside deer meat.
The smell, even the look made me feel sick.
"You're needing more sleep, daughter, are you ill?"
Grandmother was the first to note my change,
but she kept secret.
She often let me sleep, defending me
from mother's morning yells to work the fields.
Giggling girls harvested fruits in baskets,
inside my secret harvest grew silent.
A somber load I carried home alone.

Drying our food was a convenient
excuse to escape and avoid mother.
I spent much time on our rooftop thinking,
about Ezekiel, dreaming about
our time at the water's edge.
Days shortened, the cold winds that carve rock came.
Winter months are secret time spent inside
like a prison under watchful eyes.
Mother observed all my needs and actions,
her questions relentless and fierce.
"Whose seed have you brought into this village?"
Her dark brown eyes became obsidian.
"Do not lie. Who did you meet while hunting?"
My response, silence. A slap, her reply.

Each night Grandmother soothed me with wisdom.
"Why can we accept the thief of death, but
not the herald of life?" She sadly asked.
Above us whispers grew louder each night.

Old Subversions

I could feel the ill will pressing down
on me, my baby and all of the family.
Village voices smoldered outside our door.
Fueled by enmity, sharp tongues of fire
fanned gossip, burning dung smoke permeated
our lives and elders plotted their old ways.

"The hunting trip was cursed because you took
our daughter and Little Song as well,
that is what they say. Husband, you must listen!"
"The lack of deer is due to drought and not
a curse!" Father's tired and worn reply.
I feared his resolve growing thin.
He sighed, then stood tall and held mother tight.
His strength reassured her and she relaxed,
enough for one day.

Again another finely ground corn meal day.
Grandmother's nimble wrinkled fingers worked
the kernels from the husks and I helped her.
Mother worked the grind stone metate,
The effort relieved her frustrations.
The rhythm of the stone
crushing blue corn bones,
her breathing like a runner, exhausting.
"Daughter, slow down you will wear out the stones,"
Grandmother joked, her eyes never drifting
from her task. I giggled, mother glared back.
Beads of sweat, angry droplets on her face.
Her voice coarse, measured as if grinding me.
"This is all your fault, your sin and silence."

Grandmother stared and mother looked away.
"Enough! We all keep sins silent, don't we?"

After a long silence, grandmother spoke.
"Child, do you know what you are guilty of?"
I lowered my head. She lifted my chin,
gently saying, "Nothing, only the most
natural thing on earth." Her eyes welled up.

"Next week the season of Lent will begin.
Let us walk humble in the procession
to receive ashes." Grandmother stated.
Mother stood up, stroked my hair and nodded.
"We will walk with you."
Kneeling, she began to grind slow again.

The black sash fit snug around my middle
between round belly and blossoming breasts,
a signal to all that I was with child.
We walked the long procession
under skies of slate, into a church of stone
to hear Franciscan brothers clad in brown proclaim:
we are dust and to dust we shall return.

That night I whispered my secret love story,
grandmother listened.
We were two young girls sharing a secret.
Moonlight revealing her recalling smile.
She cupped my belly in her soft work hands.
We felt the baby move.
A deep peaceful sleep overcame us.

Road Runner Dance

Spring came with all its promises of green.
In return our commitment to the earth,
working our patches of ground, forming rows
like braiding mother nature's loam brown hair.

It was now mid-June. Like the days, I too,
was increasing, growing round all over.
Little Song helped me weed again.
She did most of the talking while I did
most of the weeding.

Council members and their warriors watched
from a short distance. One approached
his name, Gray Crane, his nose a bird-like beak.
He spoke of the importance of weeding,
purifying, allowing some to grow
while some is plucked like a sacrifice.
He gawked, asking if we understood.
We nodded, hoping he'd leave us alone.
As he walked back, a hot whirlwind passed
between us and them. Dust and weeds spiraled.
Little Song made a flapping gesture with
folded arms and uttered a crane like squawk.
We burst into subdued laughter.
I peed.

The year's longest day arrived, summer's birth.
Mother and father were down in the fields.
My pains grew close apart, my water broke.
Grandmother instructed Little Song to go call
the medicine woman, then run quickly

to the fields and bring back mother.
She assured us father knew the customs
and would make all the arrangements.

On the steep trail back up, mother caught sight
of Choshka stalking a snake.
Briefly they paused to watch the road runner dance
hunting the snake. Choshka hopped around
with an extended fluttering wing.
The black and white striped pattern mesmerized
the snake as Choshka danced. When the snake
struck at the wing, Choshka delivered a blow
to the snake's head. Three times they danced until
the snake was dead, it's banded skin dangling
from Choshka's beak like string.

My son was born before the sunset on
the first day of summer nineteen-o-three.
Alert with dark black hair and light brown skin,
he was beautiful, my secret harvest.
I had passed into the great sisterhood
of mothers, unaware of what it meant.

The naming ceremony required
us to prepare special corn meal dishes.
Father invited the eldest council member
a spiritual leader, ninety years of age.
Father wanted to give my son the name
Yellow Sun. He thought it a perfect name,
reflective of my name, yet symbolic
of summer solstice.
Mother spoke, telling us her story

of the road runner killing a snake
on the path and Little Song confirmed it.
The elder shaman came and held my son.
He blew breath on him and spoke his new name,
Choshka!
My son was then handed to grandmother,
the eldest of our family household.
She spoke his name, then father, then mother.
She proudly placed him in my waiting arms.
I cried for joy at all unfolding before me.

After the customary days passed,
father asked about a Christian name.
I chose Ezekiel. Surprised, they asked why?
"It's his father's name," I replied.
I told my story, how things had come to pass.
They listened intently, grandmother at my side.
An infrequent question from mother,
just to clarify things in her mind.

Journey East, September Gifts

Late summer times were warm with peace and calm,
the tensions in our home abated
by Ezekiel's birth. But the spirits
of tension and confrontation do not rest,
they seek new hosts. Divisions among
the council members kept father busy.
Up above there was whispering again.
Below my son slept safe, secure
between the warmth of grandmother and me.

From the roof top I sent up my prayers.

Ezekiel wrapped in my lap, I prayed.
I asked to see my love, my son's father.
That night the rains came filling the cisterns.
The welcomed rainstorms lasted several days.
It was a good sign.

Two Franciscan brothers walked among
the village homes asking for food donations.
It was their way. On this particular visit,
father spoke with them at great length.
I watched them from the roof but could not hear.
Their body gestures revealed true interest.
Mother brought out a basket filled with food.
She joined the conversation. When they left,
father and mother went for a long walk.

One night father revealed his intentions
to make a trip beyond the great river
to a certain village named Tomé.
I turned quickly, my heart beating faster.
My mind filled with questions then father spoke.
"It is right to negotiate a marriage.
I have here a letter from our priest,
addressed to the pastor in Tomé.
Father Rael will assist me in finding
the shepherd boy and his family.
This young man, E-ze-ki-el, I must meet."
Mother nodded and said, "We must prepare gifts,
offerings from our family to his."
I trembled, overwhelmed at what they said.
At my side grandmother grinned approval.

I collected clay for the pottery
grandmother and I decided to make.
We shaped two bowls, the smaller fit inside
the other. Grandmother said this one
is you, the smaller one represents
little Choshka, who fits inside his mother.
Smiling, we worked. While the clay was still wet
I took my son's hands and imprinted
the bottom of each bowl - our son's signature.

Preparations for the journey were made.
Father's cousin loaned him a buckskin horse,
stubborn but strong. Father kept him penned
in a corral near our family garden.
Little Choshka came with me to feed
the horse and watch it eat. My mind drifted
to my first ride on the painted pony.
As desire stirred in me, swelling slowly
up into my breast, my face flushed.
My baby felt it too, and he cooed, kicking
his feet quickly, sensing my emotions.

Our voices mingled under morning's pale sky.
Father packed the buckskin's back, while talking.
"Remember our hunting trips? They began
this way, me and you eager and packing
for each journey not knowing how they'd end."
"Yes father. They are unforgettable
special memories."
"And mine as well dear daughter, mine as well.
I want you to know I have no regrets, none."
He paused and faced me.

"Your skills and abilities are equal to men,
but you are much more, you can love."
"Father, I..., I want to say..."
His strong warm hand caressed my face so gentle.
I pulled it tight against my cheek
closing my eyes, in my mind speaking
all I could not say. Somehow he sensed it.
"Be at peace," he told me. "Events happen for a reason.
We now have a grandson who brings new hope.
Now I journey not to hunt deer, but your husband."
It was father's humor; we both smiled.
He described the route he'd take as we walked
the steep path home together.

He and mother hugged three times.
Grandmother blessed him for the journey
and he thanked her.
Lifting up his grandson over his head,
he said, "Little Choshka, I leave you
in charge of the house and all these women."
Hugging one last time, mother slung a jug
and a food-filled leather pouch around his neck.
"Expect my return in about ten days.
Daughter knows quite well the route I'm taking."

Mother and I climbed up to the roof top,
our lookout, to watch father ride eastward.
"Many times I've stood here to watch our men
leave. The past few years you, too, left with them."
Mother did not look at me, her eyes were
in the past, but her words in the present.
Words of reconciliation and hope.

"When you departed I felt alone and
angry. Perhaps what I felt was envy,
wanting to share in the experience."

There was quiet. In silence the sun rose,
the golden glow painted mother's cheek bones.
She looked beautiful as she offered her
cornmeal prayer for father's safe journey.

Casting Lots
A chain of events began unfolding.
The eldest council member, old shaman,
suffered a paralysis and died days later.
Wrapped in a blanket, as was our custom,
he was buried before sunset.
Within days a new leader was chosen,
a religious leader. His name, Gray Crane.

All the village was speaking about this.
Mother, disappointed, wished father
could have been here as he was on the council.
Grandmother must have been very tired
for she said nothing, then went straight to bed.
In the morning we heard drums, it meant
a ceremony. I took my son to watch
the dancers and listen to the drumming.
When we returned, grandmother looked worried.
"Was it a snake dance?" she asked.
I nodded, bouncing my baby on my hip.
"And the paint, the paint what did it look like?"
"Red and black zig-zags," I answered, puzzled
by her agitation.

"Where is mother?" she mumbled, pacing the room,
while a pot of beans boiled frantically,
steam rising like unanswered questions
into heaven.

An uneasy calm, a strange silence hung
over the evening. I was asked to go
see medicine woman and bring back tea.
A tea for a deep sleep. Outside our door
two warriors sat. Their bodies
painted white, zig-zag marking on their face.
The older one asked where I was going.
I told him. Then he asked about my son.
"I'm concerned, we were sent here to watch him,
make sure he is safe and secure."
His response seemed odd and out of place.
Uncomfortable, the hair on my back tingled.
I stepped back inside, my heart now pounding.
Ezekiel safely in mother's arms. I told them
of the men outside and our conversation.
I searched their faces for reassurance.
"What is happening?" I asked them again.
Grandmother held my hand, it was shaking.
"Dear daughter your son is safe with us.
Now go quickly get the tea. We will explain
everything on your return. Now go, go!"
I looked at mother and my child,
took a breath and dashed out passed the men.

On my return, my mind racing, I caught
sight of something running up the path.
A shadow figure coming towards me.

I froze, my body tense ready to scream.
It was father!
I ran and jumped into his arms.
He exclaimed, "What a pleasant welcome.
I met Ezekiel, he sends you a spe..."
I interrupted, "Father there's trouble!
Warriors are at our home. I'm afraid,
I sense an ill will towards my baby boy."
He caressed my head, looked into my face
and said, "Yellow Moon, tell me everything."
He studied every word, asking questions.
"Do not fear, we must be strong and all will
work out." His presence gave me hope, courage.
"Now, let us go home."

We took an alternate path to conceal our approach
and to view both front and side of the house.
In the dim light we could see an elder.
He directed the warriors' work
of securing ground floor windows with pine poles,
makeshift prison bars.
Father whispered, "Keep to my left then go
directly inside, comfort your infant."
Father placed himself between me and the warrior.
He spoke a loud council greeting, motioned
for me to go in while he spoke to them.

Mother sprung to her feet hearing father's voice.
I ran to my child who was in mother's arms.
Her head covered in a long black shawl.
Her voice now urgent, "Did you bring the tea?"
I nodded. She sent me and the baby

to the back room with grandmother.

Entering through the curtain, I gasped,
grandmother was on the floor, body quivering.
I dropped to my knees, shocking the baby.
Ezekiel started crying from the jolt.
Outside I could hear mother's defensive voice
Over those of the men. My mind dizzy, frantic.
Then a voice from the ground, "Daughter calm down!"
Grandmother wiggled away from the wall.
"Give me the baby and the tea," she said.
Bewildered I asked, "What are you doing?"
"Digging a hole through the adobe wall.
Now you take over," grandmother ordered.

Outside the elder informed father
of the council's actions. The lot had been cast
and it fell upon our family.
We had to provide an offering,
a human life.
The decision was binding.
I heard mother scream profanities.
I ran to the front of the house to see
father restraining her in the doorway.
Outside the warriors waiting, watching.
Father motioned for me to come to mother.
He whispered, "Listen, listen, I'm going
to divide them. Force one to take me
to the Kiva and protest the decision.
They will not reverse it, but it will buy time,
maybe two hours. Then they will return.
Woman, look at me. For them to agree

I'll propose one guard wait inside,
create a false sense of security.
Woman, find a way to get them out."

The older warrior yelled out, "Enough talk!"
Father's whispers quickened, the message urgent.
"Daughter, the horse in the corral, take it
and ride to Tomé. Take the path I've shown you.
Ezekiel and his family await."
Mother spoke, "Husband, go, we have a plan."
Father nodded and embraced us. His strength
gave us courage. He went outside
and began his discussions while we plotted.

Dark Night, Magenta Morning
The moon, only a thin sickle of hope,
slowly sank toward its new moon beginning.
Tomorrow's darkness would be absolute.
Inside, our kerosene lamp glowed hope.
Mother on her knees carving out adobe.
Grandmother's conversation, shadow whispers.
"The lot has fallen on us. They mean to
feed your infant to the ancient serpent."
I gulped in disbelief, my hair tingling.
"I thought that was a legend, a story
to scare children. How do you know it's true?"
Grandmother's face turned grim, stiff like death.
"The snake's real, have no doubt.
It's kept secret and fed rabbits, chickens.
It's head the size of a dog's,
with molten-copper colored eyes.

It is old, the scales around its mouth
and on its head, have grown out like thick gray hair.
It's length that of a man from tip to tip
and the girth like a man's thigh.
And when it eats ..."
She stopped, covering her eyes with her right hand.
Aghast, I whispered "How do you know all this?"

The corners of grandmother's mouth turned sad.
Her breaths became shallow.
Mother stood and came to her side, head bowed
and placed her arms on grandmother's shoulder.

Grandmother's measured voice, "I know, because,
fifty years ago, my infant, was taken."
A muffled scream rose from inside my throat.
I pulled my bundled child closer,
my heart pounding into his sleeping face.

The voices of men entering our home
dragged us back into the present danger.
Mother quickly went out through the curtain.
Grandmother concealed the hole with the bed.
Father's voice beckoned us to come out.
Mother stood out in front of us, guarding.
Inside, the elder and warrior stood behind father.
"They must see the baby before they agree
to escort me to meet Gray Crane tonight."
Father's voice serious and deep.
The elder cautiously walked forward.
Instinctively, mother and grandmother
positioned themselves around the baby

like buffalo protect their calves from wolves.
I clutched my child against my pounding chest.
Slowly the elder extended his hand as if to touch
my precious child with death's hand.
Cat-like, mother lunged, scratching his left cheek.
"You've seen enough!" Mother flashed her teeth.
He whirled away, touching his face, feeling blood.
The warrior sprung forward to aid him.
Father pivoted quickly between us and them,
holding up his hand, commanding, "Stop!
You've seen the child, now uphold your word,
and escort me to the kiva at once."
The elder's voice broke the silence.
"Let us leave them now."
He scoffed at mother.
Turning to the guard he ordered,
"Stay alert, be watchful and bar the door."

It was a standoff for several minutes.
"We are going into that room to sleep.
Sit by the door, do not dare come in," mother warned.
Her words were sharp like a flint chipped edge.
"No! You all stay here where I can see you,"
the warrior countered. He stood firm.
I felt a cold sweat and my legs tremble.
Grandmother shuffled forward, speaking out,
"Would you allow a man in your house
to watch over your women while they sleep?"
The guard quickly scanned our faces, thinking.
Mother grabbed the mano from the metate.
Holding up her weapon she declared,
"We are going in there now."

"No, no," the warrior shouted back.
Pointing at me he commanded,
"You, take the baby to the upper room
put him to bed then come back down here."
I began to panic. Grandmother fell
into the table clutching at her heart,
groaning in pain. Mother quickly took
Ezekiel from my arms and commanded,
"Help your grandmother to her room,
she is sick from all this worry."
She looked at me and pointed with her lips.
I knew what she was thinking.
I acted quickly, lifting grandmother, escorting her
through the curtain as she repeated,
"My heart, my poor heart cannot bear all this."
"See what you've done to her!" mother scolded
as a mother scolds a guilty little boy.
"I'll take the child and put him to bed.
Then I'll come down and join them in the room."
The guard now feeling in control agreed.

Behind the curtain, grandmother whispered,
"Quickly child, kick out the mud plaster.
But wait till I moan loudly. Once outside
your mother will lower your infant down."
Knowing I might not see her again,
I began to weep. Grandmother cupped my face
in her soft work hands. "Saving your child
has healed me of an old, old wound. Now go."
She kissed and blessed me, then began to moan.

I crawled through the hole. Above me

mother was waiting. She lowered my baby down
through the narrow window with a cord
made from braided hair. Both my mothers had cut
their mantels of strength. Two generations
of beauty woven, now used to lower
my son down from a starry sky into
my outstretched arms.
"Go quickly, daughter you have my blessings.
We'll see each other again, rest assured.
Run, save your baby."

Determined, I sprinted into the night.
My heart pumped energy through my veins.
I felt as though I was being hunted.
Village dogs barking.
Enveloped in darkness, I ran down the path.
Long strides, legs pounding on the downhill slope.
Approaching the corral I heard a horse stir.
No, there were two, one a painted pony.
It was Estrella! Ezekiel's gift to me.
Panting, I approached, her ears pricked forward.
She nuzzled at the baby in my arms,
then uttered a soft maternal nicker.
I spoke, "This is little Ezekiel."
She replied, a gentle snort, I'm ready.
I mounted her, my baby securely strapped to me.
With one hand I held her mane, mantel of strength.
My other arm wrapped around my child.
Estrella trotted, I leaned forward,
she folded back her ears and accelerated
into a full run.
The feeling of speed exhilarating.

My hair flying in the night air like dreams.
Each stride separating us from danger,
and bringing us closer to love's embrace.

She galloped for two miles then cooled down
to a walk that lasted hours.
Finally my son awoke from the tea-induced sleep.
On horseback I nursed him, the stars watching.
The late September night dew brought a chill.
Mother's black shawl our only covering.
Slowly eastern skies went from indigo
to blue, then a glowing magenta morning.

At the Rio Puerco we stopped briefly.
I located water and cleaned my baby.
I looked back in the direction of home,
Estrella puffed, her vibrating nostrils said,
come I know the way, a new home awaits.
It was passed mid-day, the grassy plains had come
to a jagged end.

From the mesa's edge we looked across a
magnificent river valley of green.
Tomé's landmark, a black volcanic hill
mutely greeted us. I took in the sights.
The wide cottonwood forest and marshes;
cultivated fields and further still
grass-covered gravel hills and beyond them
a chain of blue mountains which father
had shown me once before on a hunting trip.
Somewhere down there my new life waited.
The pains of the previous night gave way

to unexplored hope. I gently gigged my
painted pony. Estrella began her
slow descent into the river valley.

Epilogue
Ezekiel married me. We began
a wonderful happy life together.
Father remained a council member,
blame for my escape placed on my mothers.
Ostracized, they moved outside the village.

The serpent died in nineteen twenty nine.
I imagine there was relief among
most mothers and their clans, except
for those who clung to hurts and craved revenge.
Two years after the snake's death, my family
moved to a ranch south of Grants to care
for my aging parents.

In total we had five healthy children,
four strong boys and finally a precious daughter.
My husband gave her the name Consuelo
in honor of my grandmother who
gave me so much comfort and relief.
When Consuelo reached age twelve, her father and I
took her hunting for the first time.
She rode Estrella's foal.

Conclusion
The sky now indigo over the West Mesa.
Me in deep reverie, solitary

staring out my window, the bus stops.
The driver speaks, "It's the end of the route."
I thank her and ask, "Do you think this bus
has the colors of a painted pony?"
Puzzled, she ponders and asks, "What do you mean?"
"A horse, the colors, are those of a horse,
and you are the rider," I tell her.
"I guess, why not?" She smiles, door opens,
 I step out into reality
and the glow of a full moon.

FIVE
Going Home

Route #222-5, Precious Cargo

For Steven

Memories like sand, abundant, abrasive
pass through the hourglass
each grain helps pass time
on the afternoon drive.

Sleep, a brief pause at the end of a paddle board.
Unconscious ending, to the next day's toil
alarm clock rings at four AM.

Take Time Out To Be A Dad

Reminds the billboard on Gibson Boulevard.
It's sad we advertise to make some men behave.
Yet, good dads do what they must.

Driver's thoughts turn to Sky,
he shares her hot fries.
His son on his back, a quick horsey ride.
Daughter's new trepidations
that come with sixth grade.
His precious three are near, they sit well behaved.

My memory flash back,
to when I was twelve.
Dad took us to work a couple of times
in the back of a contact delivery truck.
In the pitch black cargo hold,
me and my brother rode
reclining on piles of Christmas post.

At the end of dad's run
we helped him unload.

Back in the present, I smile at the scene
three little passengers tanned by the sun,
brown almond shaped eyes like their dad.
Older sister sits in the middle, wears glasses.
On either side, a sibling with toys.
Above the sounds of the engine and city
dad listens and smiles when they say something silly.

Their father carefully works on his run.
The weather outside, gentle, and calm
like their dad. He's at peace
for his cargo is near him. He's at peace
when his children are with him.

ROUTE #54, LAND SCAPE HERO

For Roger

Neck, chest, and arms, strong and shaped
Not from dead weights at a gym
But from yards of soil and sand
Lots of board feet moved by hand
Hands that shape land and tame trees
Arms that wrestle rail road ties

Toil in the sun makes him bronze
All the skin you can see, bronze
Cheeks and nose tip a buffed bronze

Brown hair waves out from his cap
Locks, from the sun, fade to blonde
Thick hair and cap like a mat
To rest his head on the glass
Spent, he will sleep in the seat
The cool bus ride home, a treat.

ROUTE #250, THREE PEAT

For Donna

Ride the rails
        Pen some verses
Roll on rubber
        Think them over
Ramble to work
        Imagination
Return trip back
        Do it again.

ROUTE #2, GOOD BEAT, EASY TO DANCE 2

For Eric and the music of the 60s and 70s

Windows feel the bass, wipers keep the beat,
D. J. Erick in the seat
of this mobile band stand bus.

A forty-foot long console record player,
polished wood grain Magnavox,
black vinyl record tires spinning

funk and disco, rock and soul, a steady
flow of hits, rolls down Albuquerque streets.
Feet tapping wait in line to board the jamming bus.

Bell bottoms ring while Motown sings
in black and white keys of complex
harmonies. Rhythms rise and fall

men and women bump and hustle.
Clothes and smiles glow in black light sweat.
Down the center aisle a disco ball beams spots.

It's one long joy ride all night long.
Everyone gets down, but no one pulls on
the stop requested cord on the band stand route.

ROUTE #5, IF YOU FORGET

For caregivers of Alzheimer's and dementia

Faraway stare, a care giver
gets off at ninety-five hundred
Montgomery Boulevard.

Slow rewind, erase.

If I come out wearing
blazing polyester pants
and over them Depends,
smile, walk me back, change me,
 treat me with respect.

Somewhere on my memory reel
there's a clip of you at two
wearing cotton underwear
over blue pajamas,
superhero uniform.

I let you run and save the world
then watched you fade away to sleep.
It's my turn now, to fade.

Slow rewind erase.

My face remains, the rest is going blank.

Route #6, Sprinkled Spice

For Simi

Oriental sounding nickname,
he came to Burque from LA.
Works a split, the five and six,
on mornings runs drives to the train.

Enjoys water melon, loves the smell,
eats a big, red, juicy slice
sprinkled with red chile powder.

Passenger wearing a black hat,
standing, looks a bit unsure.
In the mirror, driver reads his face,
and asks him where he's going.
Man just smiles and nods.

Driver asks again, but sprinkles in some Spanish.
Muchas gracias black hat replies.
Stop requested, the man steps off,
jogging, wearing pointy boots,
Walmart bags dangle from his arms.
He makes his bus connection.

A little spice goes a long way.

Route #93, Arroyo del Oso

Mouth stained red from Cherry Hills
grunts out words in Tanoan.

Sharp claws learned to play
classical guitar at the Academy.

Black bear charging down the canyon
like rumbling flash flood rain.

Paw prints leave behind
quarter-million dollar homes.

Sipping beer on golf course greens
two under an eagle, three over a bear.

Cubs, not too far away
ride the rides at Cliffs until

a westward breeze at evening
carries spirit bear up canyons.

Route #12, Brass Ring

Evergreens: piñon and juniper
grow outside our window.
They sway in the wind
and cool in moon glow
together - apart.
Landscaping, paid in part
by overtime wages.

We need a new T.V.,
        I pick up an extra route.
Let's go out and dance.
        I need to crash out.
We share a bed
        but not our dreams.

It seems the band around my finger
is wearing thin. I'm striving
for a new brass ring.

At gatherings people say,
You two look ok.
Evergreens die slowly.
                I'm working late again.

Route #162, Ventana Views

For Gilbert

There are windows, views of town,
and seats from which to watch our city.
Drama, humor, Academy to Zuni, every street
a stage, our southwest sun
provides the mood and colors.
The sun, herald of each season.

Time, the changing seasons
are reasons for celebration across town.
Nature and people wear seasonal colors
like costumes on parade down Central street.
Above it all, our friendly sun
shines unprejudiced warmth on the city.

Golden glow warms duke and drunk alike in the city.
Lawyer or loiterer all share the seasons.
All citizens under a Zia sun.
From uptown to down town
a sunset paints everyone on the street
their own unique color.

Bus riders, skin tone colors
palette of brown, residents of the city
beautiful people fill the streets
to celebrate fiesta season.
Tourists and locals dance in old town,
all rainbow children of the sun.

Music plays, mountains blaze red in setting sun
and vivid fiesta colors
decorate the gazeebo in Old Town.
It's a party for the city.
Summer time is fiesta season
so come celebrate in the street.

Along many residential streets
in the absence of winter sun
luminarias represent the Christmas season.
A simple yet spectacular sight of color.
Thousands of candles transform the city
into an earthly galaxy around Old Town.

View our city through bus windows as it changes colors.
The high desert setting and rising sun paints every streets.
All across town it's a harmony of light with each season.

Route #51, Ode to Carll

In memory of Carll Swing

He feared, and often said, that he'd get fired,
but never. He was a good driver.
On time to work even an hour early.
Reliable, heartbeat of a city bus.

Grumpy, a rough exterior, a defense,
his only defense against some people
getting close, encroaching on his space.
The face he wore to be a public servant.

Yet, his was a kind smile, tucked away behind
a beard of responsibility grown caring
for mother then dad, he the youngest son.
This World Is Not My Home, his favorite hymn.

Black gloves, barrier between man and machine,
slight hunch back from life pushing down, down.
Glasses, strong prescription magnified blue eyes
that did not like to see people being mean.

So close your eyes
You can close your eyes it's alright
I don't know no love songs
And you can't sing the blues anymore
But I can sing this song
And you can sing this song when I'm gone - Songwriter James Taylor

Route #7, New and Improved

For Felipe

Primordial soup comes in a can.
It's got a warning label and instructions.
Empty contents into pan and apply energy.
In four billion years you'll have guests for dinner.
You have been warned, they may subdue and eat you.

ROUTE #92, CHAIN RESTAURANTS

Rolling billboards, buses display
giant images, all you can eat
pizza, Chinese buffets.

Chain restaurants they're called.
Chains, are customers slaves?
Corporate recipes, clones
of glossy menu images.

Prepackaged kits delivered
in refrigerated trucks.
Thawed and prepared behind
swinging doors by immigrants.

Tattooed wrist, proficient smile
serves the sizzling dish.
Torpid customers folded
into corner booth

consume the mounds of
gluten, meat and salt,
reflection of the picture
on the end of a chain.

Route #217, Secret Serpent

For those who work on Kirtland Air Force Base

On the test site there are places
where few people go,
must have a need to know.

In bright light, from a distance
the long chain-link tube shimmers
guanine skin of a great sea serpent.

Concertina wire dorsal fin.
Red block buildings
desert corral reefs
the oarfish stretches between.

Sea serpent sentinel with
black dome eyes on posts
knows that I'm approaching.

At the end of the chain-link body
a remote metal gate, gapes
I hesitate, swallow and step in.

Route #101ˢᵗ Airborne

For Tio Joe, a Korean War paratrooper

There is no bus route on Tramway Boulevard,
but if there was, it would be route 101.
It would start at Central
then head north.
The bus would slowly rise into the sky
up, up, up like the tram.
The city down below a mosaic of spots.

Bike rack up front holds
hang-glides.
Riders pull the stop chord.
Rip chord.
Static line.
Back door pops open.
Cold air RUSH.
Go, go, go, go, go!

Passengers jump,
parachutes deploy from lunch boxes,
purses and backpacks.
They slowly float down,
land around neighborhoods
form a perimeter
then walk home for dinner.

ROUTE #157, UPTOWN WITH MOM

For single moms

The buzz and hustle,
school lists in hand.
They're out of supplies!
Monsoon skies threaten.
Rows and racks,
of fall semester clothes.
Shop, try them all on.

A break from the crowds,
all the buzz and hustle.
We rest close together
sharing sweet treats.
Frappuccino, yum, yum,
but even more sweeter
is a day spent with mom.

Route #366, Silver Dollar Jackpot

Route 366 runs from the ABQ RIDE Central & Unser
transit center to Route 66 Casino

For Damien and all teachers

It shimmers like silver, in the desert it's gold.
The drought so old in New Mexico,
water is bought and sold.

But, the other day
we hit a jackpot
driving across town. At first the sky
paid out only in dimes, little drops
that splat
        against the windshield.

Clouds rolled in quadruple sevens.
We hit the big one!
They opened up and dumped.

Silver dollar rain drops,
cold hard cash
            splashed down on the city.
The streets flowed silver,
and arroyos
        overflowed with the payout.

Route #777, Davis Gun

For Chris

The first recoilless cannon
was designed during World War I.
The Davis Gun, named for its creator.
Twin barrels arranged back-to-back.
Twin hemispheres of the brain,
we can train to heal or kill.

Propellant charge placed in the middle
fires in opposite directions,
a gentle palm caress or solid fist to the face.
Targeting of the gun is precise
delivering words that slice through deceit
or praise honesty and good behavior.

The Davis Gun has two barrels
like right and left strong arms,
can offer alms, embrace or *chingasos*.
On the great seal of America, the eagle
holds arrows and olive branches.
Your actions decide what you get.

Route #100, Out of Service - Something in Nothing

For Vernon

It's the presence of nothing that make some things standout.
Intrigue and enchantment, the senses fill in what's missing.

Vailed headdress reveals only a slice of face.
It's the covered space that draws in the imagination.

Gapped tooth smile, a bit of nothing there
we stare at the pleasant nature of the grin.

Fashion, the art of where to remove fabric and skin conceal
the deficiencies combine to define style and attractive.

Thousands of Grand Canyon tourists
will insist on selfies standing at the edge of nothing.

The immense emptiness of a night sky
makes me try to see spirits in the stars.

ROUTE #17, SUNSET CARRIAGE

For Billy

There is a commuter leaving once each day.
It crosses town, just before sunset.
People come from all quarters of the city.
White bikes loaded on its rack.

I tried to ride it once, but it was full
of *viejitos*, cancer patients and unborn.
I saw Johnny Tapia get on
along with my brother and son.

Rising over the Sandias,
climbing on golden thread
as the sunset paints the mountain red.
All aboard, our beloved dead.

Ever skyward, before leaving the atmosphere,
their memories descend
as multi-colored sparks, butterflies, tear drops, silver rain,
to ease our pain and bless the land again.

Amen

Alvarado Landing Strip

For Mark

Model Shoe Shine Parlor,
family owned at 224 Gold Street.
The best place in town
to view buses coming in
for a landing
at day's end
is an elevated shoeshine seat.

Resplendent amber sunset.
Buses land on golden runway
then taxi in
to Alvarado station.
I watch pilot friends
cruise in,
thankful for their service
to la *gente* de Albuquerque.

I pray as they come in to land,
often tired and alone.
Felt cloth snaps, my shoes now shine
like the beacon sun
            that guides them home.

SIX
Mid-September Mourning

Mid-September Mourning

Life was work and then there was his job – often 12 or 14 hours. Joe accepted life as it was. He'd been raised that way by grandparents. No secret formula, but basic principles grandfather counted off on his left hand: faith, honesty, hard work, determination and show up early. This is how the family for generations had overcome adversity and not just survived, but prospered. Joe knew this. He'd been battling adversity head on for years, working and caring for his sick child. However, when it ended it came fast and was strangely wonderful.

ଔ ଔ ଔ ଔ ଔ

It was the last run of the evening, just past 8 p.m. Nature's display unfolding over the West Mesa captured the driver's gaze. A crescent moon sank slowly through a palette of blue and pink. Beautiful, the perfect arc of reflected light was like her smile. His foot relaxed off the accelerator and he coasted into the comfort of the past. The moon became her smiling face, red and beaded in sweat from her great effort.

"It's a boy!" The nurses moved about quickly in the delivery room.

"You did it! You did it natural, no drugs. You're wonderful." Joe kissed his wife's swollen hand.

Pin drops of sweat across the top of her broad lips glistened like dew catching rising sun light.

She turned to face him, eyes glazed. Her smile a perfect crescent. "A boy, a boy, no drugs," her whisper became a smile again.

A nurse's voice announced across the room, "APGAR score is a three, maybe four."

"What does that mean?" her smile dimmed.

The newborn was placed under an oxygen tent.

Joe caressed her hair. "Everything will be ok."

A distant voice called out, "Back door." Now two voices, "BACK DOOR!"

Joe's mind skidded back into the present. His left hand mechanically reached for the rear door lever. The last two sober riders got off near the Warren South Apartments. One of them called out, "Thanks driver." Joe nodded, then switched his gaze in the mirror to the man slumped in the rear seat. Joe valued sleep and let the passenger enjoy a few more minutes.

The bus turned onto Gibson, the orange header board now read "GARAGE". At Yale he turned north, proceeded a little then stopped near the city park. Unbuckling, the driver headed to the back. Pausing near the sleeping passenger, the driver hissed, "ffiss," like the sound of air brakes. He examined the sleeper: pants dry, good; no drool, OK. The man's long black hair, like the mane of a mustang, lay across his left cheek. A stained Dukes baseball cap bridled the wild hair.

Tapping him firmly with his strong left hand, Joe, the driver, said, "Ok, time to get up." A second time a little louder and harder, "OK sir, this is the last stop!" Coming to, the rider slowly staggered to his feet. "Groggy but stable" thought Joe. "Come on brother, this is the last stop." Joe helped him safely off the bus and pointed him in the direction of some good trees that provided a bit of shelter and privacy. Just then bus 329 passed on its way to the garage. Two short honks and one long, Joe recognized it was his good friend Rodger passing.

Back at the transit center, Joe met up with Rodger in the break room.

"I saw you doing it again. Why do you even let those guys ride?" said Rodger.

Joe hissed, "ffiss, better on the bus than in an alley. For some it's the warmest cheapest motel in town", Joe said in jest. "Besides, you know they're harmless."

Rodger knew his friend had a big heart. It was his strength and sometimes his weakness, too. "They aren't always harmless. Drunks can cause problems for the other passengers. You know that."

"If their pants are dry and they can walk on and pay, I let them ride, same as the rest of the public. It's my bus. If they start trouble I handle it."

"Yeah, and that's what gets you love letters my friend."

Love letters, what the drivers call the written complaints. Joe had a reputation for getting love letters.

There was a pause in their conversation as each man shuffled through papers. In the background, sounds of drivers chatting mixed with the occasional crack of colliding billiard balls from drivers releasing stress at the breakroom pool table.

Rodger began a new conversation. "So, did you pick up another route tonight?"

"Yep, Little Central again," replied Joe. A busy route, the San Mateo skirted some of the poorer neighborhoods of town, lots of wheel chair requests and working class. It was dubbed Little Central because of the clientele.

Jason crashed the conversation. "So, Hoser, driving Little Central again? How come you like those crappy routes?" said the familiar voice from a nearby table. Jason enjoyed bantering, even provoking Joe. For Jason it was a verbal boxing match and he considered himself the champ. Joe, as well as others, found it annoying.

"The same reason you pick up extra routes Jay, the overtime! Ffiss," hissed Joe.

"Yeah, you know you drive those routes searching for your druggy wife, bro! Maybe she'll get on your bus with some gang-banger at one of the drug stops. What will you do then, bro?" Jason's question was just bad bait. He stood there wearing dark shades, big biceps crossed over his chest, waiting for a reaction.

Rodger's eyes scanned over quickly to see Joe's left hand clench in a fist. Joe's anger rose up like the foam in a shaken soda bottle.

"Let it go man. It's just Jason," counseled Rodger.

Joe hissed like a boiler letting out some steam. His anger ebbed. Yet, he realized there was some truth to Jason's crude remark. Joe was on the lookout for his wife Angel; he had been for some time. He had not seen her in over five years. Albuquerque is big with lots of places to hide. Joe knew the dark world of heroin and meth addiction is distorted, desperate, and ugly at best and he often bid on routes that went through or skirted the less desirable areas of the city: the war zone, and the South Valley. There were times when he drove routes hoping he'd see his lost Angel.

He still loved her. He never divorced her even though she had abandoned him and Sammy. In Joe's mind his wife lived as she once was; a beautiful down to earth girl with an extraordinary smile. He held on to those memories, threads of hope that she'd get better and come back to their son. He believed in her.

"That's your problem Jay, you have low expectations of women. That's why the lady drivers think you're an asshole!" Joe said, slowly standing up. His response landed a left uppercut.

"I may be one but you smell like an ass. Clean up, take a shower man. We have a dress code, remember bro?" Jason let out a flurry of verbal punches. "Your beard is shabby, you have B.O. and you look like you're 60," Jason barked as he left the room. The round was over.

"What a jerk," said another driver.

People continued chatting and playing pool. It was a typical end of shift afternoon in the transit center break room.

ᘓ ᘓ ᘓ ᘓ ᘓ

Twenty miles south, Joe's sister Nancy waited at a gas station near the Isleta Casino. The car was easy to spot, a beat up blue Oldsmobile that burned oil and a plywood cover in place of a rear door window. It was Zeke's car and his brother Matt was with him. They were Angel's crazy cousins. Their nicknames were Zero and Minus One, a reference to IQs. Friends and family just called them Z and Minus.

Nancy smiled and gave them a friendly wave as they pulled up, a faint blue smoke coming from the tail pipe. Unlike Joe, she'd always maintained good relations with Angel's side of the family, not so much because she liked them, but because she was nice to everyone. She was "buena jente" good people. The brothers got out and greeted Nancy.

"Long time no see – Nancee," said Zero poetically. He was wearing a blue Pit Bull cap, a little hologram sticker still on the bill. The dark blue Dickies shirt he wore hung down almost to his knees. Nancy and Zero exchanged a quick hug as Minus waited his turn.

"Oralé, Nancy. You're looking fine." He hugged her with his tattooed sinewy right arm.

Minus looked like an old hound dog, brown and lanky with big ears. The blue bandana he wore down low on his head pushed his ears out, making them look even bigger. He sported a thin black mustache that curved down low onto his chin, giving him a droopy look.

Nancy replied, "He had to work, but he's glad you could meet me here. Sammy is real sick and we were hoping you know where to find Angel. She needs to come see Sammy at UNM Hospital. Do you know where she is?"

Minus nodded yes while Zero answered, "Angel she don't want nobody to see her. She is trying to come clean. She's staying in our chante now (chante, slang for house). You can tell Joe that."

"Well, how is she? What's her condition?" Nancy needed more details.

Zero answered, "We took her to the clinic and the doctor gave her medicine to help her with the withdrawals. She'll be OK. Our mom is taking care of her real good."

Minus shook his head and chuckled, "She's skinny, cuz the meth man got her butt. Ijolé, and her teeth look like corn nuts, but she's strong. Mom says the demons have to come out of her before she'll let her go anywhere."

Nancy's mouth frowned gently in compassion. She understood the struggle. The trio talked for about 10 minutes. Then Zero, looking anxious, asked, "You don't have no money for gas?"

Nancy held up her hand. "Just a minute." She pulled out a large box of groceries from her back seat. "Joe sent you this." It was a kind of peace offering. Zero scanned the box and handed it to Minus who went through it like a dog searching for a treat.

"Right on, beef jerky." Minus had scored. "Remember when Joe would go elk hunting and then Angel would make a lot of beef jerky? That was the best, esé," reminisced Minus. His brother nodded in agreement. Nancy grinned, and in her mind chuckled wondering how one turned elk meat into beef jerky.

Both Zero and his car were in need of a drink, bad. "Can you put us some gas, Nancy? We drove a long way to meet you. I'll pay you back for sure."

Joe had given his sister $30 with instructions to not tell the brothers it was from him. Years ago Joe vowed never to give them money. Nancy gave half of it to the brothers in gas and the rest in cash. The brothers were grateful. Nancy thanked them for meeting her and said she would be praying for Angel and them, too.

Some people resemble their pets. Zeke, he resembled his car; both wore blue, both smoked. Zeke was bald and so were the car tires, and both were guzzlers. How they kept going was a mystery. Shaking her head, Nancy watched them drive away heading south on Highway 47. She had a lot to tell her brother.

CR CR CR CR CR

Back at the transit center, Joe and Rodger continued their conversation. Rodger sipped on a Pepsi and asked, "How is Sammy doing?"

"We had a good day," Joe said. "I told him stories like always. He ate a little more today than yesterday. That's always a good thing."

"Did Sammy ask for his mom?" Rodger asked the hard question.

There was a short pause. Joe looked far away for a moment before answering, "Yes, yes he did. I told him the usual, that she's sick and will come when she's better."

"So, how's that coming, you know, trying to find her?"

"Well, the whole family knows we're looking for her. I know she cares about Sammy, but she's still mad at me, at herself, at everything and doesn't want to be seen. She just doesn't care about herself." Joe shook and hung his head.

"Wrong, Joe! She's a drug addict and her habit controls her, man! You have to stop blaming yourself about what happened years ago. You did the best you could. You couldn't be with her 24/7. The drug demons from her past just came back when she was vulnerable and she back-slid. It wasn't you Joe. She had issues. You're a good man and you take good care of your boy, her boy."

Children enter the world as a spotless crystal. Parents only leave finger prints, at best. Angel, she was a shattered crystal; a third generation drug addict. Broken can be fixed, shattered is a forlorn puzzle. Her family stifled Angel's natural abilities and talents. Never nurtured, constant negativity, only her physical beauty received any attention, often unhealthy. She gave into anger and grew to believe she was deserving of nothing good. It was hard for her to love because she did not love herself. Joe had been the best thing that had ever entered her life and she ran away from him, believing she did not deserve good things.

Joe pulled from his wallet his prized possession, a photo of his beautiful wife. He looked at her image, then passed the photo to his friend. Rodger had seen it before but he studied it anew.

"She's certainly pretty. To me she has an Anne Hathaway smile."

Joe sighed, "That face, it was her blessing and a curse."

"What do you mean?"

"Her smile and beauty were a magnet, too powerful for her to handle. It attracted everything, good and bad and for a simple person it's easy to be deceived. Angel loved simple things - nature, fishing, making jerky, back packing and just being outdoors. She was strong and yet weak. I was attracted to her inner qualities more than her good looks and I fell in love with her," Joe explained as he took the photo and gave it a gentle kiss. The two friends sat, silently thinking.

Stroking his beard, Joe asked, "Do I look 60?"

A smile came to Rodger's face. "You slept in the truck again, didn't you?"

Joe looked down and nodded.

"You are a little ripe today my friend and your beard could use a trim. Other than that, I'd say you look 49." The friends laughed and went on their way.

൚ ൚ ൚ ൚ ൚

The last five years of Joe's life had an accelerated aging effect on him. The stress of a child with cancer, and an absent drug addict wife took a toll. On top of all that, he carried a heavy work load to cover the cost of medical bills.

Joe was 33, but looked older. Physically he was strong and even stronger mentally. Joe stood 5 feet 10 inches and weighed 200 pounds. His features were New Mexican, light piñon skin, thick black hair, brown eyes with a hint of green. Compassionate and round, his eyes protruded slightly. Dark pouches under his eyes testified to his lack of sleep. On a good night he slept five hours straight, if all went well.

One sanctuary from life was his sister's one bedroom apartment. Joe helped her with rent in exchange for an occasional home cooked meal and a place to shower, sleep and change clothes. She was his best friend, a confidant. He visited his sister Nancy every Sunday, his only day off. Joe's stamina came from his heritage and upbringing. Having lost his parents in a car accident when he was eight, he and his sister were raised by grandparents in northern New Mexico. From grandparents Joe learned his faith and to love life and the land. He also learned to live simply, work hard and be respectful. More than anything Joe loved nature and the outdoors. Hunting and fishing were his passion. The mountains rejuvenated him, but he'd not experienced their healing atmosphere for a long time. Bus driving was a good job and it kept him in town close to his son and his second home, the hospital.

ೞ ೞ ೞ ೞ ೞ

Birds singing woke Joe up. It was his phone alarm set for 4:20 a.m. He sat up and gave his face a good long rub. He focused across the room at the monitors above the hospital bed. All seemed normal. Clearing his head, he checked his phone for messages.

"Yes!" he said to himself. The text from his sister read "clean shirts & pants in truck." The next message read, "saw 0 & -1, need to talk about Angel"

He quickly typed a reply. He loved his younger sister. Their strong bond had been forged by their parents death years ago. She always came through for him and he helped her however he could.

Stepping onto a cold floor his toes curled up as he walked to his son's bed. Sammy looked like porcelain the iridescent glow of the medical instruments gave his skin a blue hue. Joe kissed his left thumb then gently traced a cross on the forehead of the sleeping child.

The night nurse entered and whispered, "There is some fresh coffee here for you." She looked at the little boy sleeping and turned to Joe, saying, "He had a good night."

Joe smiled, nodded and tip-toed into the bathroom to shower and get ready for work.

ଔ ଔ ଔ ଔ ଔ

The Friday morning route was uneventful, routine. Finishing up the morning split, he headed back to the hospital around 8:30 a.m., the whole time exchanging text messages with his sister.

His five year old son was sitting up in bed holding the toy deer when Joe arrived. Joe smiled and called to him as he entered the room with a bag of cookies, "How's my big Sampson today?"

"Daddy!" the weak child turned and smiled, his swollen red gums, like cinnamon sticks, and his bright brown eyes were stark contrast against his pale face. Those eyes were a reflection of his mother and Joe loved to see his little boy's face.

"Hello, Joe," said Anna from behind the desk. "Come see me after story time."

Joe gave a little wave and nodded. Anna was the charge nurse for the oncology floor and Joe's friend.

The dedicated father asked, "Ready for some stories?" Sammy looked forward each day to story time with his father. For the bed-bound child it was play time. The tales filled with the colors, sights, and smells of nature came from Joe's life experiences in the mountains, hunting and fishing. If possible, Joe would take his son up north. As it was, Joe could only bring the mountains to his son through the stories.

There were many but their favorite told of the camping trip to the waterfalls, the most treasured memory in Joe's mind and heart. Through this tale Sammy knew his mom for he did not remember her. The only image Sammy had of his mother was painted by his father's brush on the canvas of the child's mind through the water-fall story.

On that waterfall camping trip, high in the Pecos Wilderness, Joe and Angel committed their love to each other. Below Sheep's Head Peak near the falls and under the stars is where they conceived Sammy. This sacred memory was a great gift that sustained Joe through the difficult and turbulent years that followed.

With his 26-pound pound child in his lap, Joe began. "Your mother loved the mountains as much as me. She was strong and could carry a heavy backpack for miles. It was mid-September and the trees in the higher elevations were beginning to change colors."

Sammy interjected, "Yellow like the desert grass, orange like the sunset, and reddish brown like my mom's hair."

Joe nodded and went on. "The trail going up through the pines smelled like lingering incense in church. Your mom would stop to admire a tree for its size and shape. She would describe it in different ways. Then I'd see it through her eyes. Your mother liked trees." Joe paused. "Her brown eyes could see beauty in the forest that other people could not.

"When we reached the falls we set up camp. I went and collected good firewood and stones for the fire pit. Your mom started setting up camp. She picked a good spot and carefully unpacked our supplies and equipment. She knew how take the food and hang it from..."

"Daddy, you forgot the part about soaking your feet," Sammy said, knowing the narrative.

"Yes, I forgot." Joe backtracked in the story. "After the long hike up to the falls, we would first go soak our feet in one of the cold water pools. It felt so good and it gave us the energy to set up camp." At this point in the tale Joe would take some water and wet the bottom of Sammy's little white feet. He would also wiggle his toes and gently massage the boy's skinny legs. Often Sammy smiled and sometimes giggled despite the pain that emanated from his bones. This little game was a father's way of checking his son's circulation and to be silly, too. After a few minutes of foot fun Sammy would get dad back on track.

"And the trout daddy, don't forget the trout!" Sammy refocused his father.

"Me and your mom would sit quietly at the edge of the pool. She would snuggle into my arms so close I could feel her heart beat and hear her breathe. We'd sit quietly, then she would see the trout and whisper, 'over there' and point with her lips; her beautiful broad lips that were the color of café con leché."

Joe paused, deep in his thoughts, holding on to the sweet memory of his wife's beautiful face looking up at his and then a gentle kiss and then another. Sammy looked up at his father and smiled and snuggled into his father's chest, bringing him back to the story. "The fish, they were cutthroat trout with their distinct sprinkles. Your mother was good at catching them, too." Joe paused anticipating his son's next question.

"Why did God give them sprinkles?" Sammy asked his usual question.

His father answered, "To make them unique among all fish. That's how our Father the Creator shows his love, by sprinkling a little bit of heaven on his creation."

"Like the spots on my belly?" said Sammy.

"Yes like the spots on your belly and the spots on the baby deer, lady bugs, and on the owls of the forest." Joe gave Sammy a little kiss and continued. "At seeing the trout your mom would smile big and I loved to see her beautiful teeth. They were like snow white perfect pebbles, smooth and clean in the bottom of a stream." Sammy would then show off his little perfect teeth. This was now time for a treat.

Often Joe brought in cookies with sprinkles, of course. He and his son would eat one together. Nausea was a constant unwelcomed companion for Sammy. Joe was happy when his son ate half a cookie. Joe would hold Sammy in his arms close enough to feel him breathe.

Sammy nibbled on the sprinkled treat as his father continued the story.

The hospital room was situated so that the morning sun entered the window. By 10:30 a.m. the sun light in the room began to dim, obscured by the adjacent hospital wing. Joe sensed the light change and knew story time was ending. Sammy, in his father's arms, relaxed into a deep sleep.

Anna stood in the doorway listening, observing. She often listened to the stories. Quietly entering she helped Joe put the sleeping child to bed and in a soft voice said, "Sammy was alert for a long time today. He should sleep well. He likes to hear them over and over, doesn't he?"

Joe smiled and nodded. He looked at the time on his cell phone and hissed. "Ffiss. I better get going."

"That's what makes children so wonderful," Anna said. "They like to do things over and over again. Take little Rachel over there. She loves to swing. I swing her in my arms and she says 'Do it again, do it again.' "And I do until I can't anymore. Do you ever get tired of doing it again Joe?"

Joe shrugged and said, "I think God is like a kid, never tiring of doing it again and again. Like the sunrise. On my morning routes when I see the sunrise I think, 'yes, he did it again.' "One more day for me and Sammy."

"That's so beautiful," replied Anna, her small hand gently rubbing Joe's arm as he leaned on the counter. "Joe, Doctor Pearson has test results he needs to review with you." Her hand now firmly gripped his forearm.

ભ ભ ભ ભ ભ

Dr. Pearson was a tall man with a salt and pepper beard and friendly demeanor. He'd directed Sammy's leukemia care the last two years. He and Joe met in the usual place to go over the latest test results. However, this time no options were discussed. Instead the conversation focused on end of life preparations. Joe faded into his thoughts and memories. A strange chill spread through his body.

"How long does he have? Joe asked bravely.

The doctor shifted slightly in his chair. His lips formed a slight pucker. He looked directly at Joe and said, "One week, maybe 10 days. Sammy is very strong."

Joe let out an "ooff", like a boxer taking a hard body shot.

Never had the walk through the hospital seemed so long and cold. Joe made several phone calls, the first one to his sister. He asked her to contact family. They agreed to meet at the apartment. Joe called Ron Perez, his supervisor, explained the situation and took the afternoon off.

A retired Army master sergeant, Perez told Joe, "Chavez, you do what you need to do. We have protectors here to cover your run." Protectors are on-call drivers who pick up routes as needed. Joe's regular day off was Sunday and he also asked for Saturday off. It had been months since Joe had two days off in a row. His body and mind needed the rest.

ભ ભ ભ ભ ભ

Sunday morning Joe accompanied his sister to 8:00 a.m. Mass. The first scripture passage read was from Isaiah, Chapter 53, "a man of sorrow and acquainted with infirmity and suffering."

The words seemed to speak directly to Joe about his son. Sammy's young life spent mostly in hospitals. Countless needles, probing and often painful invasive procedures. The tears that welled up dripped down into his beard. Noticing her brother, Nancy slid closer to him and taking his hand cried with him. It was a cathartic experience for both. Eyes tearing, Joe recited a four word prayer, "God please help me."

The walk from the church to the apartment was quiet, it had a calming effect. A cool morning breeze caused leaves to flutter in the morning light, reminding Joe of air rushing down mountain canyons. He smiled and held his sisters hand. After breakfast Joe went to the hospital. He spent a pleasant day with his son. In the wheelchair they cursed the hospital and even snuck outside and told a story under the trees. It was an amazingly good day. Joe slept calmly that night on the couch bed in Sammy's room.

ଓ ଓ ଓ ଓ ଓ

Joe's Monday morning arrived at 4:20 a.m. as it had for the last two years. This Monday was the beginning of a new bid route. He drove his first one way of the morning anticipating the sunrise. Some drivers complained about sunrise and sunset because of the glare. Not Joe, he welcomed it. The bus approached a stop where a group of people waited in the cool morning. One rider began loading a bicycle as others boarded. Joe was looking at his paddle board, learning the route when the bike rider got on.

"G'morning," said a women, swiping her bus pass. Joe glanced up, his heart rate jumped and the back of his neck tingled. His wife! He uttered a muffled "What?" His mouth opened as his head swung around to watch her walk back. "Pffho!" he exhaled, clearing his mind and shaking his head. He quickly shifted his eyes to the rear view mirror to watch her sit.

His left hand mechanically reached for the lever to close the doors. He failed twice, pushing the wrong direction. It was an awkward moment. The usual bus riders attributed the awkwardness to "new driver syndrome." Joe checked his mirrors and finally pulled out into traffic. His mind was racing with wonder and memories. He watched in the mirror as she removed her bike helmet and freed her hair. Except for some golden highlights, her hair was the same color, texture, and length as Angel's. This girl seemed more refined and composed. Her skin was a little lighter than Angel's, too. He concluded it was not his wife, but the resemblance was striking. "What's going on?" he wondered. Were his memories and emotions conspiring against him?

Distracted by his thoughts, Joe miscalculated the traffic light causing him to hit the brakes hard. Riders lunged forward. Sleepers awoke and a backpack spilled its contents, a lunch slid down the aisle. "Crap!" thought Joe.

"Brake check!" a heckling voice came from behind.

"What a bad first impression," Joe thought. He hissed "ffiss," regaining his composure and road concentration. One of the regular riders changed seats, sitting closer to the driver.

"New route for you?" he asked politely.

"Yes." Joe acknowledged his side-seat driver with a nod. It was better they conclude "new driver syndrome" than "he's checking out the chick." As the route continued, he occasionally checked out the mystery girl. She wore a black sports top trimmed in blue with matching pants. From her neck hung an ID badge and on her back an Osprey day pack.

"You've got some dips coming up," advised the co-pilot. Joe nodded. An intersection with two successive dips was fast approaching. Joe adjusted his speed. "Her bike!" he thought. Slowing almost to a stop the twenty-ton bus gently crossed the intersection. Joe wondered where she'd get off.

"Stop requested," announced the electronic voice. Standing up, the mystery girl made her way to the front. She had an athletic build similar to Angel's, but slightly taller, maybe 5 foot 5 inches. Joe's body tensed, feeling her presence so close. The bus stopped, she said "Thanks" and nimbly got off.

Joe watched through the huge windshield as she removed her bike from the rack. At the last moment she made eye contact with Joe and flashed a beautiful smile signaling "OK, good to go."

Joe's eyes opened wide. She has a powerful smile like Angel's. Joe's mind raced with thoughts.

During one of his breaks, he called Rodger and told him about the mystery girl and the morning events. "So what do you think?" Joe asked.

"Well, you've been under a lot of stress lately and it might be wishful thinking. Joe, you may be seeing what you want to see," Rodger postulated.

"So you think I'm seeing things? I tell you I slept great last night and my mind was clear this morning when I saw her."

"I don't know, they say everyone has a look alike in this world. Maybe you found Angel's double. Let's see if she rides tomorrow and maybe you can talk to her."

"Well, of course I want to see if she rides again tomorrow, but a conversation? I don't know how that would happen. This girl is kind of sophisticated. I'm not in her league." Joe replied realistically. Just then an anxious, complex idea entered into Joe's mind. He thought to himself, "If I could talk to her, then maybe..."

That night neither Sammy nor Joe slept well. Sammy battled stomach cramps and Joe was anxious, his mind swirling with ideas.

ଓ ଓ ଓ ଓ ଓ

Tuesday morning, Joe was nervous as the bus approached the stop where she got on Monday. His keen eyesight spotted the white bicycle from a distance. She was there. He tried to be discreet as he watched her load her bike, paying attention to every detail. The bicycle was a Cannondale, a high end model. As she boarded, Joe said "Good morning, welcome aboard." The greeting caused her to momentarily pause and take note of him. In the morning light, Joe's eyes sparkled green and friendly. She tilted her head slightly, an inquisitive body posture, and said "Good morning to you, too." She swiped her bus pass, smiled, then walked back to sit. Joe recognized her ID badge as one issued by the New Mexico Department of Health. But he could not make out her name.

Joe drove the route flawlessly, sure that even Mr. Copilot was pleased. As the route continued, he occasionally glanced up to look at her in the mirror. He thought about Angel and Sammy and the wishful notion in his head. As the bus approached her stop, she came to the front, standing just behind the yellow floor line. Joe said to her, "Be safe on that bike. Hope to see you tomorrow."

"Thank you. You have a safe day, too." She got off at the same stop as the previous day near the auto dealership. Joe watched as she unloaded the white bicycle. When done she looked up and made eye contact. Joe gave her a big smile and waved. She waved back.

At the transit center break room Joe and Rodger sat off to the side trying to come up with some conversation starter. Frustrated, Rodger said, "Fine! Go ask some of the lady drivers what to say since you don't like any of my suggestions. I'm off tomorrow so call me if you need to talk."

Rodger headed home for the day. Joe, got ready to go spend a few hours with his son at the hospital. Sammy's condition was deteriorating. His internal organs were beginning to shut down. Joe was running out of time. He called his sister and shared his idea with her.

"It's a desperate idea, Joe. It will never work. First of all you don't even know her. Second no honest woman is going to want to pretend she is some sick kid's mother, Joe. Forget it! I mean it's not going to happen." Nancy made her point. Joe knew she was right, but he could not let go of the thought, the hope, his prayer.

ଔ ଔ ଔ ଔ ଔ

Wednesday morning, she was waiting with her white bike. Joe combed his hair with his hand and swallowed the breath mint in his mouth. He tried to make eye contact but she was preoccupied. "Good morning," he said. She gave a polite smile, swiped her bus pass and sat in the co-pilot seat. Joe couldn't believe it. He felt his heart beating faster and he broke out in a nervous sweat. He tried to swallow but his throat was dry. His body had redirected all fluids to sweat glands. There she was, an arm's length away, leaning forward feet over the yellow line.

She was still wearing her helmet. Her body posture indicated she was going to get off soon. It was now or never. He had to find out her name. He turned nervously to his right but before uttering a word, he saw her name clearly on the ID badge dangling from her neck. Mia, her name was Mia A. Roberts. He felt his face flush. He looked over his right shoulder again as a confirmation. Her name was Mia. A calming sensation overtook him. Now relaxed, he leaned to his right and asked, "Getting off soon?"

"Yes, I need to catch the 31 today."

"OK, Wyoming. That's about 4 blocks ahead and your connection will show up in about 5 minutes." Joe said confidently.

"Thanks for the information."

"You're welcome, Mia." There, he had done it, spoken her name. Mia turned toward the bus driver her eyebrows furrowed. Joe motioned to her ID. "Your badge," he said.

"Ah, yes," Mia said, nodding.

At the end of his route Joe called Rodger and told him what happened. Joe's mood was upbeat as he headed to the hospital for story time with Sammy. His mood was short lived. It was not a good day for his son. New meds made Sammy groggy and his little body swelled with fluids.

Life on autopilot seemed to describe Joe at times. His arms and legs seemed to work one job while his mind worked a second. And so it was that Wednesday afternoon. On Louisiana just south of Lomas a young man wearing a Raiders hoody stood waiting with a bike. As the bus came to a stop, Joe noticed the bicycle, a white Cannondale. It was Mia's bike, he was certain! Adrenalin rushed through his blood. He unbuckled his seat belt ready to spring his trap. The thin man, breathing heavily, boarded the bus. He began dropping coins into the fare box. Fifteen cents short, the hooded rider asked , "Can you front me some change?"

Joe rushed him like a bouncer on an unwelcome guest. His bigger body forced the thin man to step back off the bus. "Get off my bus! You're high and can't pay!" boomed Joe.

He began cursing vehemently at Joe. For about 30 seconds it was the Jerry Springer show outside the bus.

"That's my F#*%ing bike you SOB!" yelled the angry young man.

"You stole that bike! You're a thief; the cops are on their way! Get the hell out of here before the cops come!" threatened Joe, standing in front of the bike rack. The thief backed off, still cursing and flipping off Joe. When the man was a safe distance away Joe boarded the bus.

The bus was silent, a few passengers wide eyed, others uninterested. Joe hissed, letting out some steam. Tension faded, the route continued. A smile grew across Joe's face. He had Mia's bike and needed to find her and return it. This had happened for a reason - so that he could talk to her. He bounced in his seat with hope, his prayer.

He radioed in, explaining he had an urgent situation that needed immediate attention and requested a protector pick up the rest of his afternoon run.

Joe knew Mia worked for the New Mexico Department of Health but where? He did some Google searching and came up with a location that correlated with where she got off in the mornings. As he drove to the address he envisioned the bike route she might take and it made sense. Now confidant, he parked and entered the building. It reminded him of a courthouse because of the security checkpoint. Joe walked up to the guard desk and made his request. The guard made a phone call and minutes later Mia entered the lobby through a heavy wooden door. She recognized Joe as her bus driver, but the look on her face begged for an explanation.

"I've got your bicycle in my truck." Joe said, flashing a reassuring smile.

"You're kidding! How, where?" she excitedly asked. The two walked briskly to Joe's truck. She placed her hands on the bed and tip-toeing looked in. The bike safe and sound lay on a sheet of cardboard - her white Cannondale. She gave a little jump for joy and turned toward Joe, her smile on full bright. It beamed like 100 watts. Joe was overjoyed at the sight. He turned away because she looked so much like Angel. Memories flooded his mind, his heart pounded. His throat went dry.

"How did you find it?" Mia asked as she looked at the bike again. Joe retold the story in detail, pointing out the time and place where he encountered the thief.

"Oh my gosh!" she exclaimed. "That was right after the bike was taken from the restaurant." Mia explained what happened to her at lunch. She met co-workers at Padilla's Mexican Kitchen and the bike was taken from in front of the restaurant. She reported the theft to police, but figured she'd never see it again. "This is so wonderful, how can I repay you?" Joe tilted his head to gather his thoughts.

"I can write a letter to your manager or get you a gift card to your favorite place. Just name it."

Joe took a deep breath and adjusted his stance. Raising his head he made eye contact and began his request. "You have a powerful smile; a smile that can heal." Joe continued providing some details about his son's condition and prognosis. He mentioned the stories the child enjoyed hearing. He then began to explain the situation with Sammy's mother.

Mia threw up her hands. "You want me to pose as his mother?" she said, shaking her head. "I don't even know you!" she folded her arms across her chest.

"He has never seen his mom," Joe said. "I mean she left us when he was a baby. Sammy only knows her from my stories. I have described her to him many times and you have an amazing resemblance to his mother." Joe paused, breathless, head hug. "He is dying and I want to grant him this gift more than anything. And me finding your bike, I mean, it's a sign." His eyes and the lines in his face spoke "Please."

"You mean he has never seen his mother, not even in a photograph?"

Joe shook his head. "No, there is only one photo of my wife and I have never shown it to him. It's a long story and I'll tell you all of it if you'll do this for my son."

Mia studied Joe's face. Everything she saw said Joe was an honest father who loved his son. In her mind she thought, "Everything happens for a reason." And there was no denying the turn of events leading to this moment; this decision point. Mia crossed her arms and shifted her body weight back and forth a few times like a scale weighing two quantities. She brought the palms of her hands together and raised them to her face. Looking at Joe, she smiled and said, "Okay, I'll do it. I will help you, but with conditions. I will not lie and say I'm his mother."

Joe agreed, and he and Mia shook hands. A heavy load had been lifted and Joe's body relaxed. His eyes welled up and in a slow somber voice he said, "Thank you Mia. Thank you so much."

"I can't believe I'm doing this," she thought.

Mia agreed partially because of the bike circumstance and also because of her line of work. She understood the suffering of cancer patients. Mia was a cautious yet trusting person. She saw in Joe a father willing to do anything for his child and she respected and trusted that quality.

"When do you want to do this?" Mia said.

"Soon, we need to work quickly. My son's organs are failing. I'm taking tomorrow off. Can you meet with me and my sister? There is much we need to discuss."

Mia nodded in agreement. "OK, we need to prepare." She pulled a pen and pad from her lab coat and wrote down her phone number. "Call me tonight so we can work out the details for tomorrow."

ଐ ଐ ଐ ଐ ଐ

Joe and his sister arrived at the diner 30 minutes early, a habit instilled by their grandparents and reinforced over the years by work experiences. Joe fidgeted in his seat thinking what he would say. Nancy, excited, kept an eye on the entrance, eager to see this mystery girl who would help her nephew. Mia arrived wearing black jeans and a plum colored long sleeve Polo shirt. Nancy spotted her immediately. "Oh, my gosh! That has to be her, right?" she said, pointing towards the door. Joe looked up and smiled. He raised his left hand and got Mia's attention. She approached, composed and confident.

Standing to meet her, Joe said, "Mia I'd like you to meet my sister Nancy."

Mia gave a slight smile. "Nice to meet you Nancy," as she extended her hand.

Smiling warmly, Nancy took Mia's hand with both of hers. "It's so wonderful to see you in person. Thank you for coming, for helping my brother." Nancy was pleased at what she saw. Her big joy filled smile pushed her red cheeks up toward her brown eyes. At last she released Mia's hand.

Joe hissed anxiously and said, "Well, let's get started. This is the only photo I have of my wife Angel." He laid it on the table and slid it in Mia's direction. Upon seeing the picture Mia raised an eyebrow and nodded. Yes, there was a resemblance. Joe explained how all the others photos were destroyed by his wife in a rage. Nancy confirmed the crazy story and added that Joe's computer, along with many other things, had been stolen by Angle to support her habit. The computer contained lots of photos. Joe then slid over his cell phone and showed Mia pictures of Sammy. Mia's first impression was the child's round bald head, like a honeydew. He had a happy face with handsome brown eyes.

"He's a beautiful little boy," Mia said sincerely.

Joe's story unfolded neat and linear in the beginning then, like life, became complicated. The narrative became a maze with turns, side passages, back tracking and dead ends. Mia was a good listener, intuitively asking good questions. Nancy contributed details and insight from a woman's perspective.

They sat for hours. Joe talked about his military service and family history both Angel's and his. He explained how they met and the on-again off-again courtship. He emotionally recounted the water-fall camping story in great detail. The 10-day trip into the Pecos had been Angel's idea. She wanted to prove to Joe she had kicked her habit. Joe described his wife as he did for his son - her hair, smile, eyes, and her keen perception of nature. It was on that camping adventure that Sammy was conceived. Joe paused only once to quench his thirst.

The unraveling of their life began shortly after Sammy was born. "Angel blamed herself for Sammy's bad health." Deep vertical lines formed between Joe's eyebrows. "I told her so many times his condition had nothing to do with what she'd done in the past. She wouldn't believe me. I didn't want to leave her alone, but I had to go to work. That's when her old friends and family circled around like hyenas waiting to prey on the weak." Joe tightened his jaw, then hissed. These were painful and angry memories.

A loving touch, Nancy rubbed her brother's back. Joe reviewed Sammy's medical history ending with the current cancer and progno-sis. He repeated the events of the past few days bringing Mia and them together. Joe was emotionally drained. He had poured himself out for the sake of his son. Mia could see it in his face. There was silence. Joe sipped his water.

"So, tomorrow we meet at the hospital at 8:00 a.m., correct?" Mia said.

Joe nodded slowly. "Yes, that's the plan," Nancy said.

The marathon session ended and Nancy began a new conversation. Joe sat and listened. "Well, Mia now you know everything about our family. Tell us a little about you. What kind of work do you do?"

"OK, my formal training is in pharmaceutical botany. I help manage a program for the State."

Nancy leaned closer to Mia. "That's interesting. So you work with medicinal plants? Up north we'd call you a *Curandera*, a medicine woman."

Mia seemed flattered. "I moved here recently from Colorado to help manage the state's medical marijuana program for cancer patients. The need is greater than funding allows, so it's been a challenge. It's politics." Resting her hands on the edge of the table she continued. "As a hobby, I enjoy the outdoors and bike riding. I don't know many people in town yet. So, I'm glad to get to know you, even though the circumstances are, well, let's say interesting," she said with a smile.

Surprised and pleased at the information, Nancy looked at Joe and grinned. She turned to Mia and said, "A few days ago my brother called with this desperate idea about some girl who looked like Sammy's mom. I told him to forget it, but now I just think you're perfect. You are an answered prayer," she whispered. Mia tilted her head, twirled hair around her left index finger and smiled gently.

ෆ ෆ ෆ ෆ ෆ

Friday morning, Mia and Nancy chatted in the waiting room. Nancy got a text from her brother: "start w/o me, be there soon."

"We may as well go in, Joe's on his way. Maybe he got caught in traffic. This is the best time of day for Sammy because he's alert and used to seeing his dad in the morning." At exactly 8:00 a.m. the women walked through the big automatic doors and approached the nurse's station.

Anna saw them enter and said, "Is this the special guest?"

Nancy eagerly introduced her new friend. Mia was visibly nervous and the experienced nurse turned to her and said, "You are doing a good thing for this family. Don't be nervous, honey. You are here to grant a wish. This sort of thing happens all the time here for these kids. Today it's finally Sammy's turn."

Mia took a breath and said, "How do I start? I mean, am I a fraud?"

The charge nurse chuckled. "Oh honey, you should see some of the nonsense. A few weeks ago the uncle of one of the kids came in as the little mermaid, hairy arms and all." The nurse giggled and put her arm around Mia and gently led her towards Sammy's room. "You are just here to tell a story. The child's imagination will do the rest. Go ahead girl, his father will be here soon," she smiled reassuringly.

Nancy took Mia's hand and they entered the room. "Hey, Sammy boy," his aunt said, gently rubbing his chest. "You have a special visitor today." He was awake but still, his white skin now pale yellow with jaundice.

Mia leaned over the little boy and smiled. The child responded almost instantly like a flower to sunlight. "Are you my mom?" he asked.

"Who else would I be?"

"An angel," replied Sammy. "My dad said an angel was coming today."

Mia smiled softly. "Well, my name means angel. And I am here because I am better now." Mia's middle name was Angela. Nancy watched and clasped her hands as in prayer.

At the nurse's station, Anna made a phone call, she said, "OK, Joe, you come on up. They are in the room and Sammy is awake and talking to Mia." Earlier that morning Joe met with Anna and told her everything. He also expressed reservations about this contrived meeting. Anna reassured the nervous father, saying he just had butterflies. "You have done your part well, now let us women do something for you. I'll call you once they're in the room and things get started."

Back in the room Mia and Sammy were getting acquainted. Sammy studied the angel's face looking down at him. "Dad never said you had sprinkles." There was a pause as Mia processed the child's comment.

Ah, my freckles she reasoned. She felt nervous. Mia relaxed after recalling something her father would say when, as a teen, she did not like her freckles: "A face without freckles is like a sky without stars." She smiled at Sammy and touching the bridge of her nose said, "Sprinkles are like stars in the sky. And clouds sometimes cover the stars. That's what I do with makeup, see." She leaned in a little closer to the child. Sammy listened. This was new information.

His frail hand slowly reached for Mia's hair. He touched it. He felt it between his little fingers and said, "Reddish-brown like the leaves." Looking at her golden highlights, he said. "Why is this hair yellow?"

Mia answered in her gentle voice, "The trees change colors with the seasons. This hair reflects a change in me like the trees." It was the perfect answer and the child smiled big, revealing his teeth for the first time. Mia saw two perfect little strands of pearls set into swollen red gums. His smile was a gift from his mother, she thought. Her instinctive reaction was to smile back and she did.

Sammy responded, "You have snow white perfect pebbles for teeth."

She liked the sound of that and gave a subtle laugh. "You do, too. We both do. We are the same." They had connected. She caressed his cheek and gently kissed his bald round head.

Joe arrived quietly at the nurse station. Anna lifted her finger to her lips, took Joe by the arm and escorted him to the doorway.

Mia and Sammy were holding hands. "Would you like to hear a story?" The child now more responsive nodded enthusiastically. He used all his strength to try and sit up. His Aunt Nancy used the bed controls to position him.

Mia sat on the edge of the bed and began. "Well, your father likes the mountains as much as I do. He can carry a heavy backpack for miles because he's so strong and had been trained as a soldier. We walked together in the cool mountain air stopping to look at the trees. It was mid-September and some of the trees around us were already changing colors."

Sammy interjected, "Yellow like the desert grass, orange like the sunset, and reddish brown like..." he paused, then said with a smile, "your hair."

Pleased, Mia inquisitively tilted her head, and smiled. In the doorway Joe listened to the story for the first time in his life. He had told it hundreds of times, but today he listened like Sammy. Tears rolled down his cheeks. Noticing her brother, Nancy took his hand and led him to the couch. They sat and cried together as they listened. The early morning light shining into the room illuminated Mia and Sammy's faces like gilded angels.

One of the nurses walked up to Anna. "What's going on in there?"

Anna smiled, "Oh, just a little healing."

ଓ ଓ ଓ ଓ ଓ

The smell of fresh tortillas filled the one bedroom apartment. "What a wonderful morning it was," said Nancy as she rolled out the next ball of dough. Joe savored the fresh tortilla, but not as much as the morning memory of watching Mia interact with his son.

"Joe, it was like a little miracle! Sammy was so happy and Mia was so good with him. It was like..., like there was a presence. Like she was Angel, you know?" Nancy smiled, mystified yet pleased.

"It was meant to be," Joe said.

"Don't eat anymore. I want to take a full fresh dozen to Mia later today. She is such a good person." Nancy said swatting Joe's hand away from the stack of tortillas. A knock on the door interrupted the conversation. Joe opened to see two police officers. "Good morning. Are you José Ramon Chavez?" said the older officer. This was Joe's formal name.

"Yes sir, I am. What's going on officer?" Said Joe, puzzled.

"Are you married to Angel Martinez-Chavez?"

There was a pause before answering. "Yes, yes, I'm her husband." Nancy was now standing behind her brother.

"Mr. Chavez, I'm sorry to inform you, but your wife was in a car accident."

Nancy gasped, her hands snapped up to her mouth. Joe's chest tightened and his throat went dry.

"How, is she?" Joe scanned their faces.

The younger officer looked on with a somber face as the sergeant replied, "I'm sorry Mr. Chavez, she was killed in a single vehicle roll over."

Nancy's arms wrapped around her brother and she began to cry. "Where, when did this happen?" asked a stunned Joe.

"Yesterday morning on Highway 47, north of Los Lunas," replied the sergeant. "Mr. Chavez, I'm sorry, but we need you to come and positively identify the body."

"Oh my God, oh my God. Poor Angel," cried Nancy. A burnt offering, smoke from the tortilla on the stove rose like a sad prayer.

ଔ ଔ ଔ ଔ ଔ

A white linen sheet trimmed in blue covered the body. The room evocative of death was quiet, cold and dim. The police sergeant stood toward the back of the room, the morgue attendant near the head of the table. Making a subtle head gesture the attendant pointed to the body with his eyes instructing Joe to go ahead and look. Joe slowly lifted one corner revealing a face. It was the face he had longed to see, but not this way. It was his wife Angel, her cheeks sunken, deep scratches on her left ear and neck. Her dark auburn hair like a pillow of autumn leaves. Her face smooth, relaxed and at peace. There were no more lines from the pressures of life. She looked young and not even death could steal her beauty. His eyes welled up. Joe looked up at the police officer and nodded a nervous twitch. "Yes sir. It's her." The words trickled out of his mouth.

"Mr. Chavez, I'll need to talk to you one more time when you're done. I'll be out in the hall." The officer left the room.

Giving Joe some space, the attendant said, "I'll be over there if you have any questions."

Joe slowly uncovered Angel's body, stopping at her stomach. Like a piñon without a shell, gone was the beautiful brown tone from her skin. Her body pale like Sammy's. Large jet black patches of skin on her chest and arms made Joe step back. What was the discoloration? Was it asphalt embedded in her skin from the accident? Joe wrinkled his brow and blurted, "Why is her skin black?"

The attendant stepped closer and said, "The condition is necrosis, dead tissue caused by extreme trauma." Joe pulled back the other end of the sheet and uncovered her legs. There were black patches on her shins and right knee. Only slightly visible was the twin trout tattoo above her right ankle.

"What are her injuries? How did she die?"

The attendant sighed and said, "She suffered multiple fractures as a result of being ejected from the car. Her pelvis, right arm and both legs are broken and her chest crushed. She died of internal bleeding."

Joe's legs buckled. He caught himself on the edge of the table. It was surreal. There was the body that had loved him, the body that he caressed and kissed and held so close he could feel her heartbeat. There it lay, broken and cold. He covered her legs and chest leaving only her face exposed. With his left index finger he gently traced the contour of her face, stopping at her lips. Lovingly he pushed on her lips, then brought his fingers to his mouth kissing them. He closed his eyes and prayed in silence.

In the hall Joe signed papers and was given a sealed plastic bag containing Angel's belongings. A light rain began to fall outside. In a daze Joe stood looking through the glass door beaded with rain. A childhood memory flashed into his mind. He was eight years old sitting in the back seat of his uncle Lalo's car. In the rain adults under black umbrellas stood around the grave site. He remembered looking through the car window beaded with rain, not fully understanding what was happening. His aunt's voice telling him, "Mijo, when it rains it means they are going to heaven." He did not know where his parents were but was told they were going to heaven. The memory faded to the present.

The sky had opened up to receive Angel's soul. Joe began to sob. He walked out into the street and let the rain come down on him. He was like a child, lost, confused. He walked toward the nearby University of New Mexico golf course. He sat under some trees like a wounded deer waiting for death. But he was not dying, he was living and experiencing the depths of emotion that come from loving. Hours earlier his spirit had been atop Sandia Peak. Now it plunged 5000 feet into the mud of the valley below. He fell onto his side, face in the mud and curled up in a fetal position and wept bitterly. His tears mingled with the rain and the ground drank them.

Half an hour passed. The healing rain turned to sprinkles and then to Zia sun. Joe sat up wiping the mud from his face. He was soaking wet and felt cold and emotionally emaciated. He thought of himself as one of the homeless he often saw, living under trees, alone, dirty, emotionally wrecked. He staggered up, a strange sensation to pee. Behind bushes he tried to relieve himself, only to trickle like an old man with prostate problems. Joe was in shock. The sun's rays beaming through the clouds brought him back to reality and the knowledge his son lay in a hospital bed just hundreds of yards away. The thought gave him strength. He walked back to his truck and retreated to the sanctuary of the apartment. He needed to clean up and figure things out. On the drive, he called Rodger and told him about the death of his wife and the circumstances.

ભ ભ ભ ભ ભ

At the apartment Joe and Nancy went through the sealed plastic bag. It contained the clothes and shoes Angel was wearing, her tattered purse and a preliminary police report. The report indicated the cause of the accident was mechanical failure. There was no mention of alcohol or drugs. Lack of seat belt restraints was noted. Excessive speed may have contributed to the accident. The vehicle was a 1990 Oldsmobile Cutlass.

"That's Zeke's car," whispered Nancy.

The thought came to Joe that Zero would expect him to replace his car. Joe shook his head and hissed.

"He said she was trying to quit the drugs. Joe, maybe she was." Nancy looked hopeful.

"Maybe she was. I want to believe that, but...," Joe let out a long slow "fffff."

"Hey, look at this!" Nancy found a photo among the purse items.

"Let me see that," Joe said in amazement. He held it in the palm of his hand like a precious relic. The photo was one taken when Sammy was a few weeks old and had come home from the hospital. Joe's mother-in-law had come to help her daughter with the baby and snapped the photo. In the picture, Angel was sitting, holding her baby. Her big smile was joyous. Joe leaned behind her, resting his head on Angel's shoulder. His arms wrapped around his young wife. It was a beautiful picture that carried him back to pleasant times. He stared at it. His mind began sorting through "what if" scenarios. Minutes passed.

"Something's written on the back." Nancy broke the trance. It was a poem in Angel's handwriting:

> *Sitting by the stream, I wish I were a trout*
>
> *Shimmery, spotted silver, in water dart about*
>
> *Sitting in a tree, I wish I were a sparrow*
>
> *Feathery, energetic, flying like an arrow*
>
> *Sitting with my baby, all I see is me*
>
> *Trapped inside my body, wanting to be free*

Tears came gently again to Joe. "She was on her way to see her baby. I know it. She was coming to see Sammy." Joe was convinced. He handed the poem to Nancy and wiped his face. There was a long silence as they each thought about the situation.

Joe took a deep breath, his eyes closed. "Nancy, do you remember our parent's funeral?"

"A little, bits and pieces, but it's like a dream only. Why?"

"I remember two caskets side by side in the old Trampas church. It was a double funeral. Do you remember that?" Nancy shook her head and wiped her eyes. Joe scooted up in his seat and gently took his sister's hands. "I'm going to lose Sammy soon. I need you to help me make arrangements for a double funeral up in the old church." Tears welled up in Nancy's eyes again and the corners of her mouth turned sad. "We need to call uncle Lalo to help us organize everything. And our cousin Greg for the music." The rest of the afternoon brother and sister made plans and prepared for the certain final farewell.

⇒ ⇒ ⇒ ⇒ ⇒

Saturday morning came at 2:18 AM with monitors alarming. Because of failing kidneys, impurities in Sammy's blood reached toxic levels and he slipped into unconsciousness. Joe held his son's little hand while the staff worked around him.

Later that morning, Joe and Anna talked about his wife's car accident. She was shocked to hear the news of Angel's death. "I'm so sorry for you Joe." Anna hugged the devoted father. She was amazed at his emotional strength and knew that it would be pushed to the limit in the next few days.

"Joe, regarding Sammy, he may come in and out of consciousness or he may not. Listen, my experience with patients in this condition is that often they can still hear. The evidence is anecdotal, but I've seen the reactions many times." Joe listened intently to the veteran nurse. "The sense of hearing seems to be the last to go. Talk to your son. Keep telling him stories. It will be good for both of you."

"Thank you. Thank you for everything you've done, all the advice and assistance with my son. You and the staff have been wonderful. Anna, can you contact the hospital chaplain and arrange for a Catholic priest to come visit Sammy? I want him to receive his last rites."

Anna nodded, "Sure Joe, of course. And Joe, I'm going to recommend we transition to comfort measures. I'm sure Dr. Pearson will agree."

Comfort measures, Joe knew what that meant. His little boy lay still, a porcelain doll with plastic tubes coming out of him. Soon he'd be freed from the plastic shackles, the tubes removed.

Joe's head tilted, tired and drained. He stared at his child, memories swirling, time traveling, sorting what if scenarios. He took a deep breath and leaning in close whispered, "Your mom is well now. She is waiting for you, Sammy. You will be together." The father's tears rolled from his cheeks and fell upon his son's forehead. Joe looked at his son's face. The corners of his little mouth lifted. His lips parted a few times as if trying to speak.

Sammy was listening. Joe looked up in amazement to see if anyone was there to see this, but the world around them was too busy. This sacred moment was a gift for Joe and Sammy. Tears welled up again, but for joy. He wiped his nose, took a deep breath and began, "Your mother loved the mountains as much as I do." His voice was slow and choppy. "It was mid- September; and the trees in the upper elevations were already turning colors." The words came with pain and tears but he continued. "Yellow like the desert grass; orange like the sunset; and reddish brown like your mothers hair..."

ଔ ଔ ଔ ଔ ଔ

"The age that is honorable comes not with the passage of time, nor can it be measured in terms of years. Rather, understanding is the hoary crown for men and an unsullied life the attainment of old age." Wisdom, Chapter 4 Verse 8-9.

Sammy was five years and two months old. He died on a Tuesday afternoon just before sunset. He lived two days longer than the doctors had expected, proving them wrong one last time.

ভ ভ ভ ভ ভ

Out in the church parking lot family and friends exchanged goodbyes as the funeral procession formed. It was just before 11:00 a.m. A spectacular day, sunny with a few thin clouds to decorate the azure sky.

Rodger drove the lead truck, Joe in the passenger seat. On the bench seat between them were two wooden urns and some flowers. Following close behind, a Toyota SUV, Mia's vehicle. Nancy and two of her younger cousins accompanied. Taking up the rear of the caravan was Joe's uncle and cousin Greg. In the bed of his uncle's Silverado were shovels, picks and backpacks. Eight people, three generations with one common purpose. The little convoy headed south on New Mexico Highway 76, their destination, the Pecos Wilderness and the waterfall that would forever be hallowed ground. A final resting place for a mother and son.

It was a beautiful mid-September morning and in the high country the trees were changing colors.

Rodger turned to his friend who was beginning to doze and said, "Go ahead relax, you can rest now, Joe. Leave the driving to me."

About the Author

A member of the Baby Boomer generation, Dante Berry was raised by an Italian mother and native New Mexican father in the area of Tomé, New Mexico. As a child, he was influenced by his religion and the, *alabados*, song by his father. He grew up listening to the folk music, and oral histories he heard in both Italian and Spanish. He spoke the languages of his parents before learning English.

Dante married his high school sweetheart, Margaret Sanchez, and together they raised eight children. The untimely death of a son had a profound impact on him and his family and the loss informs and influences much of his writing today. Dante's travels have taken him across Europe, into parts of Mexico, and to nearly all 50 states. But New Mexico remains his home and the primary source of inspiration for his literary work. His writing reflects the beauty and grandeur of the mountains and the Rio Grande Valley as well as the diverse people and daily events of this Land of Enchantment.

Dante works for an Albuquerque-based science and engineering company. He commutes by train and bus and writes during these daily travels to and from his home in Jarales, south of Belen in Valencia County.

Index of City Bus Routes

Route Name and Brief Description

1   Juan Tabo, north/south on Juan Tabo

2   Eubank, north/south on Eubank, goes onto Kirtland

3   Louisiana, replaced by the 157 route

5   Montgomery/Carlisle, east/west on Montgomery, north/south on part of Carlisile

6   Indian School Commuter, east/west day limited runs on east side

7   Candelaria Commuter, east/west day limited runs on east side

8   Menaul, east/west on Menaul

10   North Fourth Street, north/south on 4th Street, the North Valley

11   Lomas, east/west on Lomas

12   Constitution Commuter, zig-zags east/west limited runs

13   Comanche Commuter, east/west on Comanche limited runs

16   Broadway/University/Gibson (formerly #16/18), zig-zags east/west and north/south, cuts through the city's south side

31   Wyoming, north/south on Wyoming, serves Kirtland all day

34   San Pedro Commuter, north/south limited runs

36   12th Street/Rio Grande, north/south loop through North Valley

40   D-RIDE/Free Downtown Shuttle, loop through Downtown

50   Airport/Downtown, north/south loop from Airport to Downtown

51   Atrisco/Rio Bravo, zig-zags north/south on the west side

53   Isleta, north/south route through South Valley

54   Bridge/Westgate, zig-zags east/west on the west side

66   Central Avenue, east/west the city's busiest route, the main line

92   Taylor Ranch Express, zig-zags the city east/west, limited runs

93   Academy Commuter, Downtown to East Heights, limited runs

94   Unser Commuter, Downtown to North West Side, limited runs

96   Crosstown Commuter, zig-zags from north west to south east, limited runs, goes onto Kirtland Air Force Base

97   Zuni, east/west on Coal, Lead and Zuni

98   Wyoming Commuter, north/south and then the Northwest Side, limited runs, goes onto Kirtland Air Force Base

141 San Mateo 140 San Mateo 141, north/south, one of the city's busiest routes, a.k.a. Little Central

155   Coors, north/south main line on West Side

157   Montaño/Uptown/Kirtland, zig-zags north/south and east/west, goes onto Kirtland Air Force Base

162   Ventana Ranch Commuter, zig-zags across the Northwest Side, limited runs

198   98th / Dennis Chavez, north/south on the West Side

217   Downtown - KAFB Limited, east/west to Rail Runner Station, limited runs

222   Rio Bravo/Sunport, north/south to Rail Runner Station, goes onto Kirtland Air Force Base, limited runs

250   Downtown - Sunport Express, free shuttle Downtown to airport

251   ABQ-Rio Rancho/Rail Runner Connection, west/east to Rail Runner Station, limited runs

551   Jefferson / Paseo del Norte Express, west/east, limited runs

766   Rapid Ride Red Line, Central Avenue, articulated buses, east/west Uptown to West Side,

777   Rapid Ride Green Line, Central Avenue, articulated buses, east/west Tramway to Downtown

790   Rapid Ride Blue Line, West Side to UNM, articulated buses

HEARTLINK.COM

www.ingramcontent.com/pod-product-compliance
Lightning Source LLC
Chambersburg PA
CBHW031131090426
42738CB00008B/1049